Almost a *Whisper*

A Holistic Approach to Working with Your Horse

Sam Powell
with Lane Carter

Alpine
PUBLICATIONS
Loveland, Colorado

Library of Congress Cataloging-in-Publication Data
Powell, Sam, 1942-
    Almost a whisper : a holistic approach to working with your
horse / Sam Powell with Lane Carter.
        p.   cm.
    ISBN 1-57779-026-X (hardcover)
    1. Horses--Training. 2. Horses--Behavior. 3. Human-animal
communication. 4. Horsemanship. I. Carter, Lane, 1955 -   .
II. Title.
SF287.P736   1999   99-34046
636.1'0835--dc21   CIP

Many manufacturers secure trademark rights for their products.
When Alpine Publications is aware of a trademark claim, we identify the product name by using initial capital letters.

For the sake of simplicity, the terms " he" or "she" are sometimes
used to identify an animal or person. These are used in the generic sense only. No discrimination of any kind is intended toward
either sex.

Alpine Publications and Sam Powell accept no legal responsibility
for the training methods in this book. Readers are advised to use
their own discretion and to check with their own local trainer when
making training decisions.

This book is available at special quantity discounts for breeders and
for club promotions, premiums, or educational use. Write for
details.

Cover Photos: Lane Carter
Text photos by Lane Carter unless otherwise indicated
Edited by Debbie Helmers and B. J. McKinney
Design and layout by Rudy Ramos

First printing 1999

    3 4 5 6 7 8 9 0

Printed in the United States of America.

Contents

This book is lovingly dedicated to
the memory of my father, Del Powell,
who was what I strive to be:
a kind man,
a gentle man,
a horseman.

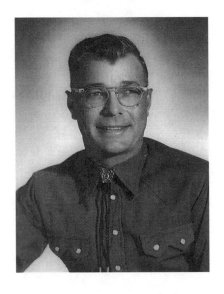

Acknowledgments

There are many people I would like to acknowledge for helping me get to this stage in my life. My gratitude to those allies and supporters who taught and encouraged me when I was struggling for knowledge and direction, and to those friends, human and animal alike, who forgave me for my many mistakes.

Special thanks to my wife and co-author, Lane, for her belief in me and what I stand for, for the sacrifices she has made to put me and this book above everything else, and for the endless hours she spent in front of the computer putting my thoughts in order and convincing me that I have a story worth telling.

My thanks to Steve and Patty Armbruster for never giving up on me and for guiding me through some very rough waters. To Terry and Carrie English for opening their home and their hearts to me whenever I was riding the grub line and needed a place to winter. To Mark Schrimpf of Bar S Quarter Horses for giving me the opportunity to work with his top quality horses and for blessing me with my great working partner, Rooster. To my sister, Jeanne Powell, for being there for me when doubts and self-destruction were pulling me under. You picked me up, dusted me off, and pointed me in the right direction, for which I am grateful. To my Dad, Del Powell, for starting me right by showing me the horse as he really is. Dad's vast knowledge was taken away too soon in my young life when I had far more questions than answers. He was all that I hope to be.

I also acknowledge all of those with whom I have come in contact personally and professionally on my journey who were willing to forgive me for the mistakes I made and the hardships I caused because of my ignorance and self-importance.

Finally I extend my gratitude to the horses themselves, who, because of their patience and forgiving nature, allowed me to learn from my mistakes and taught me to be a more understanding person.

My special thanks to Purina Mills, Inc., for their continued support and endorsement of my methods.

—SAM POWELL

There are many people in my life whom I wish to gratefully acknowledge for helping in some way to make this book a reality.

To my husband and partner in life and love, Sam, for your knowledge, wisdom and understanding, your strength, patience and persistence. You are my life. To my brother, Doug, for your determination to find the strength to maintain a positive outlook and keep putting one foot in front of the other while on your own difficult journey. You are my inspiration. To my Mom and the rest of my family for demonstrating an excitement and enthusiasm about this book that was matched only by my own. You are my will to keep going. To my daughter, Carey, for learning well the lesson I tried to teach about following your own path. You are my strength. To my son, J. J., for overcoming tremendous odds and growing up to be the fine young man you have become. You are my hope. To grandson Brandon for the knowledge you have given me about myself, and for the hours of pure, unmitigated happiness you have brought me. You are my joy. To my best friend, Kathy, for sheltering me in your home and your heart from the storms of life and for accepting me just as I am. You are my faith. To Randy DuPont, Ph.D., for helping me become the person I always wanted to be and teaching me about shades of gray. You are my confidence. To my sister-in-law, Jeanne, for sharing with me your friendship, your computer, and your vast knowledge of it. You are my stability. To the people of Hawkins Hollow—Dick, Chris, Larry, and Robyn—for giving Sam and me a place to call home. It has been our anchor.

To all of you, I extend my heartfelt thanks.

—LANE CARTER

Foreword

I have worked with horses and taught classes on horses and horsemanship most of my life. I see an increased need for educational programs for all horse owners regardless of their expertise or knowledge. I have judged horse shows and conducted horsemanship clinics in several European, South American and North American countries. Through these travels I realize that the most universal thing about horse owners is their desire to enjoy their horse as a performing athlete. All horse owners want the same thing—to know how to train their horse. Although horse owners are spending more time teaching or training their horses, they continue to use inappropriate techniques. Subsequently, the horses get worse and the owners become more frustrated.

Thank God for Sam Powell! Sam is a very unusual horseman. He not only possesses horsemanship skills and educational wisdom from years of experience, but he also is able to communicate this vast amount of information to all horse owners. Obviously, Sam is great for novice horse owners, but many of his greatest supporters are experienced horse owners. In short, he is also a talented teacher.

Sam appeals to the masses of horse owners. He can as easily communicate with a 4-H member as with a professional horseman. His techniques and concepts can be used by all horse owners, and more importantly, can be employed with all breeds and types of horses. His "Teaching by Asking" methods have demonstrated success with everything from a Tennessee Walking Horse to a mule, and from a warm blood to a zebra. Sam has always maintained that most horses are not limited in their performance ability but by the inability of the trainer to maximize the horse's potential athletic ability. The bottom line is, we limit our horses' success.

Sam Powell is able to "listen to what the horse is saying." While many horse owners complain that their horse will not listen to them, the entire communication problem may have been that the owner is not listening to or reading the horse. Using voice, touch, feel and body language, Sam unlocks that special feeling of success and love shared by horse and owner.

Sam Powell is the "real thing." His clinics, and now finally his book, are not glamour productions or fiction. His method is not based on hype and movie contracts. It is the truth . . . and it works.

I hope you can enjoy this book as much as Sam has enjoyed the experience of writing it. I want to ask each of you to really listen to what this cowboy is asking you to do. I know *Almost a Whisper* will be an important management tool for future success with your horse.

—DR. DOYLE G. MEADOWS
Professor, Horse Science
University of Tennessee

VII

Introduction

Almost a Whisper is the result of over forty years spent observing and studying the horse culture. Its purpose is to teach you, the reader, to take a more holistic approach to working with your equine friends. After reading it, I hope you will consider all aspects of horse ownership—from knowing a horse's mind to effectively managing his pasture—with the horse's natural viewpoint in mind. I hope that when you go to buy a saddle you will not just look at the pretty saddle on the tack shop rack but at how that saddle will fit and work for your particular horse. When you have a horse problem I want you to think it through from the horse's standpoint and give him the time to understand exactly what you want from him. That is what this book is about: helping you see the whole picture from the horse's point of view.

Almost a Whisper is not just another book about horses and horse training. It is a book about trust, respect, and using the art of communication to get the most out of your equine partner. It is not a step-by-step how-to book, but an introduction to an approach—a different way of thinking that will allow you to find your own solutions. I don't tell you how to train your horse in six easy lessons. In fact I don't give you a lesson structure at all. What I do give you are principles that form the basis for a solid bond of communication and understanding between horse and rider that will help you with every discipline or task you ask your horse to learn. I will try to impart some of the knowledge I've gained during those forty years of observation in a way that you can use in practical, everyday situations with your horse. Most importantly, I will help you think the way a horse thinks and understand why he acts and reacts as he does. Knowing how the horse thinks is key to becoming a real horseman or horsewoman. On that knowledge rests the success or failure of nearly everything else you do with horses.

To *whisper* means to "speak or say very softly." A whisper is very subtle, and you must listen closely in order to hear what is being said. That is a perfect description of the language of the horse and your attempt to communicate with him. It describes the manner in which many of the secrets of the universe are revealed to those who listen for them. It also describes how many of the lessons in this book will make their connection in your mind.

Horses, like humans, have a culture. They are social creatures, they fear predators, seek safety among their own kind, and desire comfort and a place with no outside pressure. Humans, believing their way is better, try to change all that. They put horses in stalls and isolate them. They feed them what they want the horse to eat, whether or not it is part of his natural diet.

They employ every training device and method imaginable to make the horse fit their own personal goals and visions, without regard to whether the horse is mentally, physically, or structurally capable of achieving those goals.

If you will take the time to understand your horse, to present ideas to him in a manner he can understand, and to earn his trust and respect, he will give one hundred percent to please you. I will teach you how to understand your horse's needs, desires, and feelings. I'll examine training situations from a horse's point of view. I'll show you how to understand and communicate with the horse's very different culture. Finally, you will look at yourself as a possible contributor to the problems you encounter with horses.

For many years I was just another horse trainer. Now, I can walk into a pen with a wild horse and within two hours I can communicate my ideas to him in a way he can understand. I can gain his respect and trust enough for him to allow me to put a saddle and rider on him without an upheaval. I allow the horse to make mistakes, deal with his fear, and work through the situation, always knowing that I will cause him no harm. However I cannot turn that horse over to his owner and expect the owner to get the same results.

Gradually, I have come to realize that only by also working with the owner can I ensure that my efforts with a horse are lasting. I now concentrate on teaching people how to work with their horse, the whole horse, and to communicate with the horse in his own language. In doing so they gain the horse's respect and trust and the training I do is much more successful.

Every time I work with a horse and help him work through a specific problem, I see a connection to a human problem. For instance, people who keep a tight rein on their horses and never allow them to make a mistake are often controlling in their personal relationships as well. The solution to their problem is not so much working with the horse as with the owner. The same simple ideas and techniques I use with horses are also applicable to human relationships. If an employer can communicate his ideas and desires to his employees in a way they can understand, the work relationship will be smoother and more productive. If husbands and wives would take the time to consider that each gender sees things from a different viewpoint and make an effort to understand the other's wants and needs, perhaps domestic violence would become a thing of the past. Every day as I read the newspaper accounts of murders, robberies, kids beating up teachers and parents, and guns in the schools, I realize that humans, for the most part, no longer have respect for one another or for mankind as a whole. Perhaps as you read this book, along with finding solutions to your horse's problems, you will also learn to communicate better—with understanding, tolerance, respect, and trust.

Almost a Whisper is designed to be read slowly, thoughtfully, and all the way through front to back. If you skip around you will miss important concepts on which other concepts are built. As you begin to put these methods to work, be patient and reward every minuscule attempt your horse makes to do it right. Remember: A journey of a thousand miles begins with a single step.

Happy whispering!

Sam Powell
July 1999

Man Versus Horse
A Cultural Experience

My father and I drove for two days to reach Montgomery Pass in the Inyo Mountains, the last sigh of the Sierra Nevadas before they collapse and tumble down toward Death Valley and the scorched Mojave wastelands. We drove across stark deserts under blistering suns and crystal starlight. We crossed powerful rivers I had only read about and refueled in nameless small towns swallowed up by isolation. I was only fifteen years old at the time and had no way of knowing that the journey would one day change my life.

The lure of Montgomery Pass was the wild horses that ran free in its canyons. I wanted to be a cowboy—to learn all about horses—so my father took me to a place where the animals lived by primal instincts and obeyed no command except the silent dictates of survival.

I had never met my father until that summer. He and my mother separated before I was born. He left Oklahoma and ended up in Scottsdale, Arizona. I didn't know much about him except that he was a cowboy. That was what I wanted to be, so I saved up a few bucks from working odd jobs after school and hopped a Greyhound bus from Bartlesville, Oklahoma, to Phoenix, Arizona. I didn't tell anyone I was going; I just left in search of the one person I figured could teach me how to be a cowboy.

It was the strangest meeting of my life. I called my dad from the Phoenix bus station, and when he walked in we recognized each other immediately. Perhaps it was because we were both wearing cowboy hats and boots, but I knew he was my father and he knew I was his son.

Dad worked for a place called the Judson School where he took care of the horses that were part of the curriculum. He was a great horseman. One of his favorite activities was to put a pack on one horse, saddle another one, and ride off into the desert—sometimes for a few hours, sometimes for a few days. Back then you could ride from Scottsdale north towards Sedona and not get into any traffic. He did that a lot.

Dad and I talked for several days and I told him that I wanted to learn

One of Dad's favorite things to do was put a pack on one horse, saddle up another and ride off into the desert.

about horses. He said that he could teach me, but that he wasn't a man given to much talk. He had tremendous patience, the kind that comes from spending time with yourself in places where clocks don't matter much. His method of teaching leaned more toward observation rather than lecture.

When we got to Montgomery Pass we camped out on a ridge overlooking a canyon the wild horses had claimed as their turf. "Watch," my father said. For two or three days he hardly said anything more.

Dad stayed busy around the campsite cooking, cleaning, gathering wood for the fire, and keeping his distance from me. I sat for hours on end staring at the horses below without knowing exactly what I was looking for. "What am I supposed to do?" I asked him more than once.

"Just watch," was his only reply.

"But I want to learn how to train horses," I pleaded.

"Watch," he repeated.

In time it dawned on me. The horses could teach me more than he could, at least for now. The hours and days I spent observing the magnificent creatures took on more meaning and I watched them with a newly discovered enthusiasm.

After several days we loaded our gear into Dad's pickup truck and drove back to Scottsdale. I wasn't sure what I had learned or how it would help me be a cowboy. Dad drove most of the way back in silence so I had plenty of time to think about it, but it took nearly thirty years for me to completely figure it out.

When I did figure out what I had learned in those early years, all of my knowledge about horses began to sort itself into a philosophy that applies just as well to people as it does to horses. I began to see the horse as I never had before, and he became something of a parable, a prism through which humanity is refracted. He showed himself as much more than just an animal, but as a being with wants, needs and desires much the same as those of humans. He emerged as part of a culture with a way of life inherently his own. A culture is made up of a group of beings that form a society. The culture of the group dictates how they live and how they raise their young. The ways of the entire group impart certain characteristics common to each individual in the group. It is possible to identify a cultural background by noting certain behaviors common to that particular culture. Observing the horse culture entails studying how horses live in their own society as its own separate entity and how they interact with each other. It means observing their way of life and their belief system and studying it from the horse's point of view. It also involves looking at the entire world as it pertains to the horse rather than to humans.

Whenever science wants to know more about a certain culture they send a team of researchers into that culture to live among the people and study their way of life. The researchers study their system of beliefs, the manner in which they raise their young, and how they interact with the world and each other. Once we are able to comprehend the instincts, customs and beliefs that differ from our own, then it is much easier to achieve communication, patience, tolerance, and understanding.

Dad tried to teach me that the horse's way of life is based on instinct—that they deal with people on an instinctive level—and he was right. Even today horses live almost purely by instinct. Their instincts to breed, to avoid harm or discomfort, and to dominate or trust the dominant herd member have been ingrained in them for thousands of years. Though the times are changing rapidly, for the most part the horse is not.

Throughout the pages of this book I will be mostly concerned with the horse's brain. It is virtually the same in all horses regardless of breed, color, or whatever other terms and methods humans have routinely used to categorize them. For this reason the information contained throughout the pages of this book will be just as relevant fifty years from now as it is today. I want to present a more holistic approach to working with your horse, a way to use what comes natural to him to achieve the results you desire and to use your mind to work with his mind.

THE HORSE AS A PREY ANIMAL

For millions of years horses have roamed the earth, slowly evolving over time into the horse we recognize today. For the sake of simplicity I won't go into great detail here about the prehistoric horse and the physical changes he has undergone over the millions of years of his evolution. What I want you to realize is that, for the period of time that concerns us here, horses are now, have always been, and for the rest of this era will always be prey animals.

The horse's eyes are fixed on the sides of his head to give him nearly 360-degree or all-around vision. His eyes are like the side mirrors on your pickup truck. His right eye sees down the right side of his body and his left eye sees down the left side, thus reducing the chance of an unseen attack. He does, however, have two blind spots: directly in front of him and directly behind him. Horses see movement very well but are not able to readily identify objects. Your horse can see a gum wrapper blowing in the breeze a mile away but he can't see a rock that is right in front of him until he falls down over it. In the horse's mind he is lunch on legs unless he remains alert to the ever-present possibility of danger. All of our many refined and scientific breeding techniques cannot remove from him that instinct which lies at the very core of his being and dictates most of his behavior throughout his life . . . the instinct to survive.

The horse's survival instinct, ingrained in him over eons in the wild, tells him that if he perceives danger he must fight or flee. Given an opportunity, his first choice will be to flee. He will run until he has established a safe distance between himself and the perceived danger. If there is no place to run, or if he perceives there is no escape, then he will fight.

Horses have two vulnerable places on their body. One is the back and the other is their soft underside. If a predator attacks them from above, they are vulnerable because it is difficult to fight off an attack from this angle. They often attempt to do so by bucking or rearing. In the old western movies the mountain lion was always poised to attack from above, from either a rock ledge or trees. Because of this vulnerability horses have a tendency to dislike things above them. Have you ever noticed where you are sitting when you ride? I personally have tried to ride a horse from just about every position possible, though not by choice. It is a whole lot easier to get your horse used to having things up above him than it is for you to try to ride underneath him. (Incidentally, he doesn't particularly like you riding there either.) The vulnerability of the horse's belly will be discussed in the last chapter.

Horses are naturally claustrophobic. They don't like enclosed places because they have no place to run if something frightens them. That is the reason a lot of them don't like to be stabled, won't enter a trailer and may react violently to being saddled at the beginning of their training program. If you will remember this you may be able to keep yourself and your horse safe when you encounter these situations until you learn how to present each one to your horse in a manner he can understand. Keep in mind that we are trying to look at the world through the horse's eyes and these fears are very real to him.

THE HERDING INSTINCT

If you watch horses roaming free in the pasture, there will always be one that seems to be in charge. In the wild, generally it will be a mare, and for the sake of simplicity here I will use the female gender when referring to the dominant horse. The dominant horse is both the mediator and protector of the herd. Because of her the other members of the herd are free to relax in the sun, play, sleep, graze peacefully along and go about their business of being horses. The herd matriarch controls almost everything. She has first choice at the new grazing area and the watering holes. In the event of the leader's death the next mare in the pecking order assumes command without dispute. It is the responsibility of the dominant mare to alert the herd to danger. She could be referred to as the "whistle blower." The other members of the herd put their confidence and trust in her. They feel safe and therefore comfortable with her in charge. Most horses are looking for just that, a place to be comfortable. You can learn to use that to your advantage.

In the horse culture, needs are simple: good grazing, water to drink, a bit of shelter and room to move about. If a horse is not comfortable in one place, he'll move someplace else. If he is standing in the sun and he gets too hot he will find some shade. Horses stand side to side facing each other's tails in order to use the swishing of the other's tail to keep irritating insects off their faces. They provide shade and often serve as windbreaks for each other in much the same manner. As you can see, to a large extent horses depend upon one another for their comfort as well as for their safety.

Horses are designed to move about and graze continuously. When not sleeping, their physical makeup dictates that they walk and graze. Horses that are kept on pasture walk an average of fifteen to twenty miles per day. We conducted a study on the ranch where I worked and discovered that, interestingly enough, so do horses that are kept in a stall all day. Horses that are kept up continuously and allowed out once a week to be either lunged in an arena, hand grazed or ridden are the ones people call me about. They can't figure out why their horse wants to run off, acts like a fool, or refuses to return to his stall.

By nature horses are very social creatures. Their herding instinct does two things—it keeps them safe and it keeps them comfortable. Horses find safety in numbers and comfort among their own kind. If you are on a trail ride and a bunch of horses goes crashing past you, no matter the reason, chances are that your horse will want to go with them. Simply put, your horse believes that the other horses have seen or sensed danger of some kind and that they are running out of fear for their lives. He does not care why they are afraid; he only cares that the last horse to run is the first horse to be eaten by the predator. You think it is the most absurd thing you've ever heard, but remember that we are looking at the world through the eyes of a prey animal. Your horse wants to go with his buddies where he will be safe from whatever caused them to be frightened. He is trying to save his life and it makes perfect sense to him. Once you begin to think like a horse, you will be able to use even an adverse situation like this to your advantage. I will explain how later on when this specific problem is addressed in Chapter Seven.

THE STALLION

Since we are talking about understanding the horse culture, I should mention here the purposes of the stallion in the society. In the wild, the stallion has only two primary functions: breeding the mares and chasing rival males away from his harem. Horse people everywhere, especially novices, should keep this small but important bit of information first and foremost in their

Photo © Kendra Bond.

minds if stallions play any part in their horse program. The stallion's instincts are breeding and fighting, period. He will do these two things before he will eat, and all of today's refined scientific breeding techniques cannot remove these instincts from him. For this reason stallions can be extremely dangerous. A stallion can maim or kill a human being very quickly. Therefore even the most well-trained, well-mannered and best-behaved stallion should always be handled only with utmost caution and respect.

Most professional breeders are continuously aware that the potential for very serious danger exists, especially during breeding season, because of the stallion's instincts. Even in a carefully controlled situation on a breeding farm, where a mare is physically taken by a trained handler to the stallion to be bred, the possibility exists that the action of that handler in returning the mare to the pasture after breeding may be viewed by the stallion as a rival stealing his mare. The stallion's instinct is to keep that from happening and he will by fighting to his own or his rival's death if necessary. Sadly, I observe almost on a daily basis those novices and some professionals who are perilously unaware of the danger involved with handling a stallion. They tickle him on the nose, allow him to push them around and nibble on their fingers and giggle at the sight of their small children playing under his feet. Try to think of things from the stallion's point of view. If you will do that, any error in your judgment of a stallion will tend to be on the side of safety rather than carelessness.

THE HORSE'S POINT OF VIEW

It is our inability as humans to look at things from the horse's point of view that causes most of the problems we encounter with them. We believe them to be dangerous because we put them in frightening situations where their instinct is to save their own lives. We believe them to be dumb animals because we are unable to communicate our desires to them in a way they can understand. We believe them to be incapable of learning anything because we lack the ability to teach them. Finally, we believe them to be incapable of feelings and emotion because we are incapable of thinking like they do and interacting with them as possessing a culture of their own. Understanding horses as comprising a culture—an entire separate existence—gives us the

Photo © Kendra Bond.

ability to view them as individuals, each as a separate but important part of the whole. Once we have changed our perception of the world of the horse we will be able to use what comes naturally to him to teach him what we want him to learn.

Humans, too, are individuals. Each is a whole within himself, but each also contributes a part to a larger whole. Human beings are, have always been, and will always be predators. Though many of our species make a conscious decision to be vegetarians, man is designed to eat meat. This constitutes the first clash of the cultures of man and horse . . . predator versus prey.

Because the horse is not capable of thinking like a human he sees you as a predator. He can't think like a human so you will have to think and act like a horse. You will have to establish yourself as the dominant member in your herd of two and become your horse's protector. This is a very important lesson for him to learn if he is to overcome his fear of you as a predator. Teach him to seek comfort in your presence, and then make sure he finds it each time he looks for it. Teach him that his life is better or more comfortable where you are and he will seek you out.

In our efforts to help make our horses more comfortable we often attempt to change everything about them that makes them horses. We begin by putting them in box stalls which restricts their free movement and isolates them from their own kind. In the human existence as punishment for crimes people are put into prison cells. Their free movement and their ability to socialize with their own kind is restricted. If additional punishment is called for while in prison it is often in the form of solitary confinement. In the human existence, isolation is nearly always viewed as a form of punishment, yet we isolate our horses and claim that it is because we love them and we want them to be comfortable and happy.

We feed our horses what we want them to eat regardless of whether or not it happens to be part of their normal diet, often selecting food they were never designed to eat. We feed them based on the recommendation of the local feed-store owner or of our neighbor down the road who may or may not have horses of his own. We seldom consider the nutritional needs of our horses and structure their feeding programs accordingly. (I have been fortunate enough to work with the people from Purina Mills who have gone to great lengths to study the nutritional requirements of the equine species and design top-quality feeds. This nutrition information is available to anyone wishing to learn more about how to properly feed and care for their horses.)

The normal diet of horses is grass, not grain. They need long-stemmed roughage in order for their digestive system to function properly. Horses kept on pasture year-round almost never have digestive problems, respiratory problems, or mental problems. That is the ideal situation for them. Horses that are deprived of long-stemmed roughage will eat the bark off trees, chew down the barn and fence posts and eat the manes and tails off one another. They will also eat grasses that they would not normally eat, some of which may be toxic to them and can result in death.

There are several good processed feeds on the market today that adequately meet the horse's nutritional needs, but thus far the equine specialists have not been able to manufacture a feed that will meet the psychological need of the horse to graze on long-stemmed roughage. My purpose is not to criticize the processed feeds; it is to teach you that horses require more than these feeds are capable of giving them, but not from a nutritional standpoint. This past winter saw a shortage of hay where I live. I was able to turn my horses out into a ten-acre pasture that had not been grazed all year. Though there was no nutritional value in the grass they were eating, they were satisfied by the act of grazing and chewing on the long-stemmed roughage. Their nutritional needs were met through a carefully structured feeding program using top-quality processed feed. People who quit smoking can often overcome the addiction to nicotine in time, but overcoming the psychological need to have something in their hand or something in their mouth is usually the most difficult aspect of quitting. If you want to keep your horse happy and healthy, but for whatever reason you can't turn him out, then supplement his diet with good quality hay year-round, as much of it as he wants, and exercise him as much as possible. Remember to feed the hay first in order to get his gut working so he can properly digest the grain and you can help ward off many of the problems that plague stabled horses.

Keeping a horse in a stall twenty-three hours a day and having him on a diet of fourteen percent sweet feed is about the same thing as feeding a hyperactive child a box of candy and locking him in a closet. It would be unthinkable to do that to a child, but we do it to our horses all the time. When I ask people why they feed their horse sweet feed, their answer never has anything to do with nutrition. They usually tell me it is because their horse likes it. I am sure he does, but that doesn't mean it's good for him. I have never seen a hyperactive child who didn't like sugar. These same people ask me to come and look at their horse because he kicked down his stall and ate the groom for breakfast. Feeding your horse this kind of diet is like putting rocket fuel in your lawn mower. He'll move pretty fast and make a lot of noise, but he has no place to go and won't get a lot of productive things accomplished. He will also burn out long before his time. You can keep your horse healthier and happier by structuring a feeding program based on his individual needs: overall health, condition, and activity level.

Our misguided efforts to make horses happy and comfortable have resulted in horses that stress easily. We have eliminated most of the horse's ability to exercise because we keep him in a stall all day. We have not only changed his eating pattern but what he was designed to eat in the first place. Standing up in a stall all day causes the horse to become bored and he begins to associate feeding time with something to do rather than with just hunger. Then if you are late getting off work and can't get to the barn at your regular time your horse becomes stressed because he is bored and hungry. He is physically stressed from the hunger and mentally stressed from the boredom. Stress, whether physical nor mental, is an underlying cause of colic in horses.

Colic is a rather vague, generic term for a host of ailments characterized by pain that originates in the abdomen. It is always costly, whether in terms of time, money or both. It is often recurrent and occasionally results in the death of the horse. Because of its insidious nature, colic is to be guarded against at all times.

Horses actually do quite well without any interference at all from humans, and we should be honest enough to admit that the things we do for them really only make us feel better. It is when we start trying to change horses to make them fit our program that we encounter problems or a clashing of the cultures. It is safe to say that all the problems we have with our horses are caused by us. These problems are indeed man-made. We employ every method and training device known to shape our horses into a realization of our own personal visions and goals, without any regard for the horses themselves.

We make no attempt to understand or even consider horses' instincts, needs, or desires as we shove them into training programs they are neither physically nor mentally ready for just because they are two years old. We think they should do all the things we want them to do because we love them and we feed them and we care for them. For us this is a valid enough reason, but all the horse knows is that he has been taken from a place where he was comfortable and put into a place where he is uncomfortable. He doesn't understand, and most of us are incapable of presenting the situation to him in a manner that he can comprehend. Instinctively he is afraid, and his fear will eventually manifest itself in the form of bad behavior, a bad attitude, or both.

This is why it is important that you look at the horse as living within his own culture and attempt to understand this culture before you can understand your horse as an individual. Understanding his culture will give you insights as to why your horse does some of the things he does. Once you begin to look at the world through the eyes of the horse and grasp the concept of his culture, you will have begun to establish an effective line of communication even before you learn to speak his language. You will then discover in your horse a much more willing partner because you will have established a relationship that is based on mutual respect, trust, and acceptable behavior. You will also become more aware of the many, many ways in which you have unwillingly and unknowingly contributed to your horse's bad habits or unacceptable behavior.

Always consider whether your horse is structurally, physically, or mentally capable of achieving the goals you set for him before you place him in a training program.

THE HORSE AS BEING

We live in a world made up of a great many different races and cultures. Having had the opportunity to travel a great deal across the country and around the world has taught me to appreciate the differences among the peoples of this planet. Each new encounter offered a tremendous learning opportunity. While I had no idea why the people of Germany did things so much differently than I, or why the Australians thought the way they thought and ate the foods they ate, I accepted these things as part of their culture without feeling that they needed to be changed. The German way of life is inherent to Germany just as the Australian way of life is to Australia. What does this seemingly illogical comparison have to do with horses? Horses, while not human, do have one important thing in common with all the other cultures of the world—they are beings.

A part Cherokee Indian, I set out in my younger days to research my Native American heritage. I discovered that many Native American tribes have no word in their vocabulary for animal. To them the animal is merely

another form of being much like themselves. Try to see the horse in this new light, as a being. That is what this book is about, helping you to see the horse in a manner you may not have previously considered. It is about changing only one thing, your perception. That alone will change everything else. Horses have likes, dislikes, wants, needs, and desires. They get hot, cold, have fears, and want to be comfortable. With your newly discovered perception of the horse, is he really all that different from you?

All through history people of different races and cultures have tried to force other people to see things their way. They believe that their way is better and therefore all others are wrong. Wars are fought over cultural differences and differences in belief systems. The white man destroyed the Indians because of differences in our cultures. Had we taken the time to observe the similarities between the two rather than focus on the differences, we might have found enough common ground to bridge the gap between the differences. Then we might have been able to come to know each other and use the differences as tools for learning about patience and tolerance rather than as excuses for hatred. The Native Americans' love of family, search for comfort, and worship of a supreme being who provides for all of their needs have the same origins in their culture as they do in ours. Yet we were unable to overlook our differences at that time and tried to make them something they were not. Expecting Native Americans to be anything other than what they are, members of their own culture, is not a realistic or achievable goal. It is just as illogical and unrealistic for you to expect your horse to be anything but a horse. To expect anything different from your horse makes as much sense as expecting a snake not to be a snake, yet that is exactly what you do anytime you engage in the use of force or violence to make your horse do something that is unnatural for him.

We think of domestic violence as cruel and barbaric, but domestic violence is nothing more than one human being using force and violence to make another act in a manner that is desirable. I am not minimizing the horror of domestic violence, but I want you to realize that the use of force is not the means to successful communication with your horse any more than it is to successful communication with a significant other. If we could only learn to accept and appreciate other humans and animals as beings first, then domestic violence, child abuse and animal cruelty might become things of the past and words to be forgotten forever.

Keep one thing in mind as you consider a change in your perception of horses. They always know more about you than you will ever know about them. In most cases they'll know more about you than you know about yourself. You can't fool horses and you can't lie to them. They'll hear what you think long before you say anything, and if what you say differs from what you think, even to the most minute degree, they'll believe what you think every time. If you act as though you've changed your perception, but you think, "This is a bunch of baloney," your horse will know how you feel and behave accordingly.

See how much of the following scenario you can relate to and perhaps you will be convinced. You go out to the pasture to catch Horse and you see the green grass, the pretty flowers and Horse grazing peacefully along. You're in a bit of a hurry because the boss kept you over a few minutes to finish an important project. He didn't know that tonight was the championship roping event. Horse, on the other hand, with his big soft eye but less-than-perfect eyesight, may see a six-foot-tall predator on his hind legs invading Horse's comfort zone with every intention of making a meal out of him. Remember the grizzly bear in the movies on his hind legs with outstretched arms about to attack his prey?

It is not important that you have a scientific knowledge about the rods and cones in the eye of the horse; it is important for you to remember that a horse sees the most minute movement but cannot readily tell what caused it. It takes a moment for him to get his head in the proper position to focus on the moving object. Because Horse doesn't identify objects well, he may think you are the grizzly bear come to eat him for lunch. After all, he senses the tension in the air because you're running late. Horse decides it is better to run well than to fight poorly, so he is off to the back side of the pasture.

You wonder what got into him as you tell yourself, "I'm late for the roping and that dumb horse is running around the pasture." You probably think he's doing it on purpose because he's stupid, mean, or just because he wants to. Fear and the horse's fight-or-flee instinct never enter into your reasoning as your blood pressure goes up and your face begins to look like the flashing red lights at the railroad crossing. You go off in pursuit of Horse thinking, "If I ever get my hands on you, I'll make dog food out of you."

Now Horse has gotten some distance away and he stops to look the situation over. He watches you come closer and tries to decide if you are friend or foe. You've gotten yourself all worked up because you're out traipsing around in the mud with your new boots on, about to forfeit your entry fee at the team roping because Horse doesn't want to be caught. Horse is thinking, "I feel a lot of hostility in the air, I sense danger—maybe I'd better leave town," and he does. It becomes a vicious cycle. As you become angrier, Horse senses more danger and becomes more afraid and even more determined to keep away from the source of the perceived danger. It never dawns on you that you are the cause of Horse's fear. After all, you have Horse's pretty, new, shiny halter over your shoulder and you are coaxing him with nice, kind words spoken through clenched teeth. The thought you had about making dog food out of him was what he heard, though, and he's not about to let you get anywhere near him.

If we are at all honest with ourselves, there is probably not one person out of a thousand that this has not happened to, myself included. The horse's confusion is the most common reason for the majority of wrecks that occur. In this situation, if you had approached Horse in the pasture with the same respect as you would have for a human friend you were visiting, you would have heard what he told you when his head shot up and his ears shot forward. The whole ugly situation could then have been avoided. You would have stopped, backed off a step or two, and apologized for invading his space and frightening him. Horse would not have felt threatened and would have stayed around long enough to focus on you and realize, "Oh that's just my owner. I bet we're going roping." In this case, as in many others, the tiniest miscommunication led to a full-scale uprising.

Learning to view the horse in this new light has led to many transformations in my personal life and my human relationships. I have studied psychology, spiritualism, mysticism, holism and even acupuncture. Students of the Eastern art of acupuncture are taught that in order to examine a patient they must do three things. They must go beyond looking and really see the patient, go beyond touching and really feel the patient, and go beyond listening and really hear the patient. Looking, touching, and listening involve only the use of the eyes, fingers, and ears, but seeing, feeling, and hearing require you to use your heart and mind as well. You are learning to observe the whole picture of your horse: his surroundings, and indeed his culture. This can start you on the path to your own personal transformation not just in the horse world but in many other aspects of your life.

Rider at a clinic held in the Australian outback.

THE IMPORTANCE OF OBSERVATION

If you really want to learn about horses, work on your power of observation. Learn to see the horse, what he's doing, and under what circumstances he is doing it. Most important, learn to see what he is telling you he is getting ready to do. What I know about the horse has come through a lifetime of observation. Perhaps that is where the "gift" people talk about can be found—in my ability to observe without judgment.

Many years ago while job hunting as a young man, I wound up in Southeast Oklahoma where I had heard a ranch was looking for help. When I arrived I found another young fellow there hoping to get the same job. The boss introduced himself and proceeded to ask us about our qualifications, if any. The other fellow had some experience with a beef-research outfit and had attended a college agriculture program. I, on the other hand, had not graduated high school and had spent most of my time trying to learn to ride bulls and broncs on the rodeo circuit. I had not been very successful at it, which is why I needed the job. But I was sure I had made the drive over there for nothing.

The boss told the two of us he had some business to attend to back at the house for an hour or so and invited us to take a walk around the ranch, the barn, pasture, or wherever we wanted to go, just to get acquainted with the place and familiarize ourselves with the layout of the land. He said he would give some thought as to which of us he would hire and tell us of his decision when he returned.

This other fellow and I wandered about the pasture, the woods surrounding the place, and the barn. The other guy was telling me all about how nice he thought it was going to be to work there. All I could really think about was what a long drive I had ahead of me to get back home and how broke I was.

About an hour later the boss came back and asked us what we thought about the place. The bright young college guy told him that he thought it was a real nice place and that he thought he'd really like working there. Then the boss asked me what I thought. I told him it was indeed a nice place but that he had a hole in the south fence where a tree had fallen on it, his pond was leaking out of the dam and it looked like muskrats were ruining the dam, and that bull nettles were taking over one corner of his pasture.

The boss looked at the two of us for a minute and then told the other guy that he sure appreciated his education and qualifications. But, he said, he did not see how he could use him since he did not seem to be able to see what was going on around him or what needed to be done. He thanked him for his time and sent him on his way.

I ended up staying there for about a year. The boss told me that to really make things work you have to be observant enough to see what needs to be done and fix it before it becomes a real problem. He said that was why he had hired me.

Grasping these simple but powerful concepts could solve many problems in the world, from working with your horse to getting along with your mate. If you will make a commitment to practice these concepts on a daily basis in all areas of your life, you will discover a kinder, gentler way of living.

It's the same with horses. By observing the entire picture, you can fix things before they become problems. If you will come to know the horse's culture, you will understand his instincts. Understand his instincts and you will understand the horse.

Horse Whispering

Understanding the Language of the Horse

Before I could reassess my approach to horses, I was forced to reassess my own self-image and how I related to those around me. For years I had been a rough and tumble cowboy who placed no value on humility, tenderness, or patience. I began to study my relationship to the world around me, the part I could see and the part I could not. The learning was profound, nearly inscrutable, close to mystical. In addition to reading everything I could get my hands on about horses, psychology and mysticism, I also read books on religion, human and animal medicine, and psychocybernetics (the study of the mind-body connection).

As I began to try to recall some of what my dad had tried to teach me long ago, much of what the horses had taught me through a lifetime of observation came back. I recalled the wild herds of Montgomery Pass and how they had maintained their tribal order. I remembered that the horse still lives almost purely by instinct. At that point I decided to figure out a way to approach the horse at the level of his instincts. I knew that if I could play on his instincts I would be able to establish a relationship in which we both got what we wanted without the use of force or fear on my part.

HOW THE HORSE COMMUNICATES

I have been observing horses for over forty years now, both in the wild and in my own pasture. Aside from my father, they have been and continue to be my greatest teachers. Through countless hours of silent watching I have learned how they communicate, or at least I have observed that communication. Fully understanding it is still beyond me. Before you can begin to understand the language of the horse, you must first appreciate his means of communication, one of which seems to be a form of mental telepathy. If one member of the herd senses danger and rears his head, all the others react instantly. Even a member of the herd that is a half-mile away and can't see the first horse's movement will react.

If you are riding your horse and become afraid, your horse knows it. He does not know that you are afraid of him; he thinks you've seen danger up ahead some place. He brings his head up to have a look around. You become more afraid because you think he's going to do something stupid, and so you do the first thing that comes to mind, which is pull back on the reins. Now your horse thinks, "Man, this person must have seen something really bad out there," and he becomes more tense. The whole situation snowballs and then the wreck happens, often in a matter of a few seconds.

A few years ago I went to Germany to conduct some equine seminars and clinics. A young lady approached me about a particular problem she was having with her horse. It seemed that whenever another horse approached them from the opposite direction as she was riding in an arena, her horse would rear up, wheel around, and run away with her. She demonstrated for me and each time the horse reacted just as she predicted. She was doing nothing to cause the horse to become frightened, at least nothing physically.

Following her demonstration she was quite shocked when I told her that she was the cause of the problem she was having. "But I"m not doing anything," she protested.

"No, but you're thinking about it. You know he's going to wheel and run and he doesn't disappoint you. It's like a self-fulfilling prophecy," I explained.

I told her that I was going to ride her horse around the arena and I was going to think the most pleasant thoughts I could think. I said I was going to get the horse completely out of my mind. After riding him for a while with the reins slack in my hand, I asked one of the other students to ride in my direction. As the other horse came towards me, the lady's horse stepped around him and walked right on without even raising his head. We did it several times in order to prove my point. Then I told her that I was going to think of something that really agitated me, really made me tense and angry. I rode over into a corner of the arena and thought about bill collectors, being stuck in traffic, and things of that nature. I got myself pretty worked up, and sure enough, when the other horse came towards us again, the lady's horse reared up, wheeled around and took off. There was nothing physically going on; it was all in my head. The horse sensed my anxiety and it made him easily spooked even though my anxiety had nothing to do with him. It's a perceptive quality horses have, something like ESP.

Later on I learned that this lady was a concert pianist and loved music. We got a Walkman radio and I told her to pick out some of the most relaxing tapes she had. We put a tape in the Walkman and she put on the headphones, got on her horse and rode around the arena for thirty minutes. During that time a half dozen or more horses passed her numerous times but her horse did not react. She was concentrating on the music, which was relaxing her; therefore her horse was relaxed.

Horses also communicate with a simple but unmistakable language. It is uncomplicated and universal. Horses all over the world speak the same identical language. A horse from Australia can communicate just as well with horses in Texas as he can with those in his own country. The language of the horse is very similar to the secrets of the universe in that it is very soft and very subtle. The language of the horse is indeed almost a whisper. Perhaps this is where the age-old term "horse whisperer" originates.

Horse whispering was once practiced by Indian Shamans and those said to have mystical powers over animals. Horse whisperer describes a breed of cowboy thought to have supernatural powers who, some 200 years ago, would take a wild horse into a private place and ride the gentled animal out a short time later. A horse whisperer communicates with the horse by mimicking the animal's natural body language. Using this method, the horse is gentled and not broken.

UNDERSTANDING THE HORSE'S GESTURES

My quest to understand the horse's view of the world led me to study and learn the nature of his instincts. Once I understood his instincts, I began to decipher his body language. What I wanted to do was figure out how to use his own language, something that was natural to him and that he could identify with, to stimulate the horse to a proper or acceptable response without the use of force, fear, or bribery as a leverage. Once you understand the horse's mind and work with it instead of against it, it's not complicated.

In the horse's mind, for example, the act of turning his rump to another horse or to you is a gesture of great disrespect. It is his way of gaining dominance and establishing himself at the top of the pecking order. Most people don't know this and they'll reach up and scratch him or do something playful like pat him or tap around back there. Right away the horse thinks he has dominated you. He's not going to have any respect for you or pay much attention to anything you try to teach him from that point on because he's the boss. He told you he was, and you did nothing to convince him otherwise.

If a horse charges at me when I walk into a pen, I'll wave my arms and charge right back at him. Is this an easy thing to do? Certainly not. Is it scary? You bet! But I don't back down, not even a tiny step to the side or backward. If I do, then he has established himself as my boss. When looking at the world through the horse's eyes and speaking his language, you realize that the little things that seem trivial to humans mean a great deal to him. Most horses, for all their massive size and brave talk, are cowards at heart. If you stand your ground, a charging horse will stop. When the horse stops charging at me, I turn my back to him and walk away. In this manner I establish myself above him in the pecking order. Without laying a hand on him, I let him know that I am not afraid of him and he respects me for it. Turning my back to him does not mean I take my eye off him. I know where he is in relation to where I am at all times.

When a horse pins his ears back or bows his neck, it's another act of defiance, a challenge to authority. But dropping the head and opening the mouth wide or snapping the teeth conveys submission. Take the time to observe a few mares out in the pasture with their babies. Anytime one of the babies does something to misbehave or shows disrespect to his mother, she will drive him out of the herd a short distance. She will make him stay out there until he submits or apologizes for his behavior. He then drops his head and licks his lips or opens his mouth wide and snaps his teeth. This is his way of telling his mother that he is sorry for being a bad boy and promising not to do it again if she will let him come back to the herd. Out away from the rest of the herd, the baby feels vulnerable. The predators can get to him easily and he's terrified. It usually doesn't take very long for him to realize that showing disrespect to his mother is a big mistake. Once he conveys his submission to her, she will allow him to return to the safety of the herd.

A grown horse will convey submission to you as the dominant member of your herd of two in the same manner if you drive him away from you for any show of disrespect. You do not have to strike him or touch him at all. Simply wave your arms at him and shoo him away. It's kind of like sending the misbehaving child to stand in the corner. You have only to let the horse know that he is not welcome to be near you at that moment. This is best accomplished in a sixty-foot round pen or small arena with no corners.

If the horse runs around with his head up, his nose stuck out and his lips tightly clenched, he is being defiant. He's like the child who sticks his tongue out at his mom because she sends him to stand in the corner. When the horse's head is more level, his lips are relaxed, and his eye has a softer look to it, then he is telling you he is ready to listen to your presentation. This is the time to approach him and say, "Listen, I have a better idea." This is the time to use what comes natural to him to help him understand that you want to be his friend and his protector, and that you aren't going to put up with any foolishness. Once you establish yourself as his boss, it automatically becomes your job to be his protector, too.

The horse has gauges on him similar to those on your automobile. His eyes, ears, mouth and the way he carries himself are all indicators of what's going on with him at any given moment. You can use these indicators to know whether he is tense or starting to relax. You can begin to judge his personality by reading these gauges. Aggressive horses will attempt to make direct eye contact with you and pin their ears back as if to say, "Get out of my space, Bud!" This is how an aggressive horse attempts to drive you away. If you go at an aggressive horse too slowly you'll get run over. A timid horse does not want to be with you, so you must work cautiously with this one. You have to take care not to do anything that will increase his fear or anxiety level because that will make him harder to convince that you mean him no harm. You must work slowly with him and encourage him to stay around long enough to figure out you are his friend.

When I went to Germany I found myself in need of a translator, as I had no knowledge of the German language or culture. I do, however, understand the language of horses and spend a great deal of time translating their language to their owners. I have discovered that the secret to fully understanding any language is learning to think in that language. The beautiful and talented singer Celine Dion was able to sing in English before she was able to speak or understand it. When she learned English, however, her singing became even more effective to the people of this country because she felt and understood what she was singing. Once you learn to think like a horse you will speak horse and speak it fluently.

LISTENING TO THE HORSE

Your horse is always talking to you. He has a quiet way of telling you things like his feet hurt, or your saddle is hurting his back, or even that he's happy and content. These may be little things but they are important. If your horse tells you there is a problem you owe it to him to listen to and understand what he is saying and then try to correct the problem.

Seek out the cause of the problem, eliminate it, and chances are the problem will go away. Anytime you attempt to solve a problem your horse may be having, take a moment to consider yourself as the probable cause. If it is a behavior problem, think about something you might have done that contributed to it. It is not fair for you to expect your horse to change unless you are willing to change too, because chances are you made him the way he is, whether you meant to or not. If you are asking your horse to go right and he seems to want to go left, make sure you are asking him to go right. I am convinced that the reason most people think their horse is goofy is because they are sending him mixed signals that confuse him. Most of the time your horse will be doing exactly what you are asking him to do whether you realize what you are asking of him or not.

One thing that age has given me is a little more wisdom. Instead of trying to physically retrain the problem horses I see, I simply start listening to them. I am then able to stop trying to figure out what the problem is because the horses themselves are telling me that. Once I stop talking and start listening, all I have to do is figure out how to eliminate the cause. It was not easy to do at first because it required me to bury my tough-guy ego and listen, as I never had before, with all of me. But from the moment I started, it got easier. Perhaps this lesson will not be as difficult for you to learn as it was for me.

The majority of the phone calls I receive are from people who seem to be having one specific problem with their horse. One of the most common statements I hear is, "All of a sudden my horse started . . . (bucking, rearing, running off, or whatever the problem)." They'll tell me that the horse had never given them any trouble at all and that he just changed overnight. Decades of observing and working with literally thousands of horses has taught me that they don't change without a physical cause and that if you learn how to listen, they'll tell you what the cause is. Many horse people think the answer to every problem they are having with their horse is to send him to a trainer.

Pay attention to details and note the timing of events that preceded any change in your horse's behavior. It could be that you found a new horseshoer because he's five bucks cheaper than the one you've been using all along. You know he's not as good as the other one, but what the heck, horseshoeing is easy, the open end goes to the back. Never mind that you're not cognizant enough afterwards to figure out that Horse's ill temper may very well be due to the fact that his feet hurt. Just send him off to the local trainer and pay a fair amount to add to the misery that Horse is already experiencing. I'd like you to try running a twenty-six mile marathon in a pair of cowboy boots that do not fit properly and see how you feel. I would be willing to bet good money that you will not be able to think about anything except how bad your feet hurt—and neither will your horse. This is not the time to try to teach him anything or to punish him for misbehaving. The answer to the problem certainly is not to send him to a trainer. The answer is to send him back to the farrier, the good one.

Maybe you found a new saddle at the tack shop and it's cheap so you buy it. This saddle doesn't fit your horse worth a hoot, but it matches your pretty new breast collar and you ride it proudly. The next weekend at the big barrel racing competition, your horse runs past the first barrel and knocks the other two down because all he has on his mind is how much his back hurts from that ill-fitting saddle. He stops just short of the far end of the parking lot and you wonder what in the world got into him as you make your way to the telephone to call the trainer, who gladly takes your horse and your money.

Perhaps you ordered a brand new bit that is a true work of art. It has

This student is thinking, trying to figure out if he should stay around and see what happens next or leave town.

engraved silver conchos and the whole works. You are completely oblivious as to what kind of mouthpiece it has or how to use it, but again, what the heck, it's awfully pretty. You go riding on Horse with your pretty new bit and it's pinching his tongue and poking a hole in the roof of his mouth. He is tossing his head and trying to tell you he's not comfortable. He is looking to you for relief from the misery because you told him you would take care of him and keep him safe and comfortable. Instead you lose your cool and jerk on the reins to try to get him to stop acting like a fool. The pain goes right through the top of his head and he rears up, loses his footing, falls over on you and breaks your leg. If Horse is lucky, when you are able, you'll go call the trainer. If he's not so lucky, you'll go call the nearest dog food plant and request a pickup. If only you had listened when Horse was tossing his head and been able to understand what he was saying to you.

A few years ago I received a call from the owner of a ten-year old gelding who told me that all of a sudden this horse started bucking people off. She said that he had never bucked before and had always been the best horse on the farm. She wanted to know if I could help her stop this horse from bucking. I went to have a look at the horse and sure enough, he could buck. By this time, age had made me painfully aware of the fact that I was no longer a bronc rider. I knew we would have to find the cause of this horse's problem and eliminate it because there would be no getting on him and trying to ride the problem out of him.

This gelding had been raised on a ranch out west. He had been roped off of, had dragged brush up and down ravines, and had had baby calves hoisted onto his back during the spring calving season. He had been exposed to just about every situation possible and was as close to being completely bombproof as any horse can get. As I watched him buck off one rider after another, I suspected his behavior had nothing to do with fear.

I buried my ego and that macho cowboy image that dominates the horse world long enough to tell the owner that I could not fix her horse. I then told her that if she would sit down with me, answer a few questions, and be honest with her answers, together we would find a reason for the change in her horse's personality. To her credit, for which I respect her a great deal, rather than telling me to take a hike and sending the horse to a local trainer, she said she wanted to find out what had happened to him.

The farm employees were brought in and questioned about changes in the horse's behavior and when they first began to notice anything out of the ordinary. One employee remembered that about six months earlier the horse had started to get a little difficult to catch in the pasture when before he had run up and stuck his nose in the halter. Another recalled that he had started to get a little cinchy and had begun to pin his ears back when he was being saddled. They had thought nothing of these subtle changes, but after a month or so he would no longer stand to be saddled at all. He would swell up when the cinch was pulled tight and become extremely agitated when the rider mounted. Still, his handlers paid no attention even though these reactions were totally out of character for this horse. The day he started bucking all they noticed was that he started bucking . . . all of a sudden.

I told the owner I was not a veterinarian, but that in my opinion, the horse needed a thorough medical exam rather than a trainer. Fortunately, in this case and for this owner, cost was not a problem. She had friends at the Oklahoma State University School of Veterinary Medicine and made arrangements to have the horse sent there to be checked. I trailered him from his home in Tennessee to OSU myself to ensure he would not be further traumatized. I told the doctors there what we had discussed back at the farm and they conducted their exam accordingly. The horse stayed at OSU for a week being x-rayed and having nuclear imaging, blood work, and a whole host of other tests done. The doctors found a torn muscle directly behind the last rib on his right side.

The owner was notified of this finding and she again questioned the hands at the barn. This time one of them remembered that six or seven months before as the horse was being led into the wash rack he had slipped and fallen. As he went down his hind legs spread out and he fell on his right side. The farm hand recalled that the horse had been a little gimpy for a day or two but seemed to get over it all right so they assumed it was nothing and kept on working him. When we put the previous discussion and the veterinary findings into a time frame the problem seemed quite obvious and made perfect sense.

The point of the story is that if anyone had listened to what the horse was saying from the beginning, he could have gotten treatment a lot sooner. When he became difficult to catch in the pasture, he was telling the boss that he was a bit under the weather and really did not want to go to work that day. However, with no sick leave in his contract, he was forced to work anyway. When the pain got worse he started to speak a little louder. Pinning his ears back was his way of insisting he just did not want to go to work. The pain became unbearable as they pulled that back cinch right up against that sore muscle, but he was kicked in the belly for swelling up and not standing still. When he finally could endure the agony no longer he got his point across by yelling. His means of yelling was bucking the rider off. The first cowboy hobbled back to the barn with his new jacket torn, his twenty-x beaver hat stomped on, aching from stem to stern and complaining about that sorry, no-good gelding that went crazy over nothing. It was only after the rider suffered a battered body and bruised ego that anyone wondered what was wrong with the horse.

Recently, I conducted a horsemanship clinic in the Birmingham, Alabama, area. The program was to consist of a horsemanship clinic held in the morning in a large arena, followed by an afternoon trail ride. There were a total of seventeen riders, mostly novices, and not a single horse that was sound enough to take out on the trail. The causes of the problems the horses were having ranged from poorly fitting tack to bad farrier work to medical and dental problems. I commend these horse people for being willing to admit they were novices and simply did not know, and that was why they had invited me there. They were eager to learn what I had to teach.

One mare in the group was so ill-tempered she pinned her ears back whenever anyone approached her. She made it quite obvious, even to these novice riders, that she did not want to be touched. Closer observation and examination of the mare revealed to me that she was sore all over and had been for quite some time. We carefully scrutinized all of her tack but that did not seem to be the culprit. The saddle was of good quality and workmanship and it fit her well. The pad was adequate, her bridle and bit were right for her, and her rider knew how to use it.

I was able to pinpoint the specific areas of her body where this mare was sore by touching her and watching her move. Time restrictions prevented me from doing much else beyond recommending that her owners have her thoroughly examined by a veterinarian. They wanted to know if I would recommend an equine massage therapist or an equine chiropractor. I told them I thought it would help make her feel better right then, but unless they could find the cause of her problem the soreness would recur. They promised to have her examined that week.

A few months later Sassy's owners called to ask if I would take her for sixty to ninety days and see if I could help her. They explained that their veterinarian had not been able to find anything medically wrong with her. I heard the frustration in their voices as they told me that Sassy was just not the happy horse they had purchased several years ago. I agreed to take the mare but only with the understanding that she would be medically examined again by a different veterinarian. They agreed and said they were willing to do whatever it took to restore Sassy to her happy self again.

Because of one area where the mare seemed to experience the most pain, I initially suspected an ovarian tumor. The test for this condition, however, proved to be negative. I reported the results to Sassy's owners and stressed the importance of their honesty with me as to her history if I was going to be able to help her. The only pertinent history they could come up with was that she had run into a fence about two years before and had flipped over backward and landed on her right side. They could not remember whether or not that incident had coincided with the change in her personality, but I suspected it did.

I studied her way of moving both with a rider and without. I paid close attention to the way she felt underneath me as I rode. Due to the amount of pain Sassy experienced during these sessions, I had to keep them short which made it all the more difficult to get to the root of her problem. Close observation and personal interaction with this mare told me she had not just one problem but several, and it was like mapping a road to try and find them. The nature of her previous fence incident gave me a starting place and we had her scheduled to be x-rayed.

The x-rays revealed an old injury to Sassy's right shoulder which was most likely caused by the fence incident. We also found her to be ten degrees off on the outside of her right foot. To get an idea of what that was like for her, put a wedge in your shoe right underneath your arch that elevates the outside of your foot. This would force you to walk around and carry your weight on the inside of your foot. Try doing this for a few days or weeks and see just how painful it is to your foot, your knees and your back. Her foot had been off for so long that, through compensating for the reduced ability to balance and the pain, Sassy's back was also out of alignment. That was exactly how she looked as she traveled and how she felt as I rode her—out of alignment. It was no wonder she had been so ill-tempered.

It took several months, several corrective trims to her feet and several visits by the equine chiropractor and the equine massage therapist to get Sassy right again. The first time the chiropractor manipulated her shoulder and back Sassy told me herself that she felt better. Her head relaxed for the first time since I had known her, her eye softened, and she just looked relieved. I believe that if she could have she would have verbally thanked all of us.

Because horses are nonverbal, you have to watch for even the most minute changes. Watch for the whisper, if you will. Those changes mean something. Don't wait until your horse has to shout before you realize something is wrong. By then it could be too late. You might be lying in a hospital bed or worse or it might simply become cost-prohibitive for you to help your horse once the problem gets to the point where he has to shout. The subtle changes that occur from day to day are your cue. Remember, don't just look at your horse, really see him. Pay attention to the gauges on your horse just as you would those on your automobile. It would never dawn on you to ignore a red oil light or an oil pressure gauge with a zero reading once you came to understand their meaning. That is what I want you to do with your horse; think, pay attention, and understand his meanings.

During one of my horsemanship clinics a few years ago one student had a rather unusual problem. Her horse was blind in one eye. She loved the horse and wanted to do everything she could to learn how to communicate with him effectively. She wanted to make his life better and seemed eager to try and understand him. She came to me and asked my advice. I gave it some thought and then I drove down to the local drug store and purchased an eye patch. I gave it to the lady and suggested that if she really wanted to see things from her horse's point of view it would probably help if she only used one eye. She was thrilled with the idea and wore the patch throughout the clinic. It gave her at least some idea as to how her horse saw things.

She had to turn her head a bit to one side in order to compensate for the loss of vision on the other side. This made her realize that her horse probably needed to do the same thing and she no longer felt the need to pull on his face and correct him whenever he turned his head to the side. She was also able to figure out that he would most likely be a bit spookier on his blind side and she would have to stand guard for him on that side so he could relax. The last I heard from her, these two were great friends and were thoroughly enjoying their trail riding adventures together. She did not let her horse's minor handicap stop them from having great fun. Instead, she used it to help her understand her horse's mind better and to develop a deeper bond with him as his protector and caregiver. She did not allow the problem to cause the horse to harm her or himself because she took the time to understand and work through it. Both horse and rider benefited from the experience.

The little changes in your horse's behavior are his only way of telling you in a polite manner that he is not comfortable or he is hurting somewhere. Listen to him. Don't automatically assume he's just having a bad hair day. While that is a possibility, you owe it to him to find out for sure. I recommend you check your tack, talk to your veterinarian, talk to your farrier, and talk to your trainer, and I suggest you do it in that order. Don't let a breakdown in communications between you and your horse fester to the point that it gets you or the horse injured or killed.

Bar S Doc's Bueno (Little Bit) and Mark Schrimpf six months after I started helping the horse learn to control his fears. Horse owned by Mark Schrimpf, Bar S Quarter Horses.

Anytime an incident occurs, it is always the horse that gets the blame. People never consider that whatever went wrong might have happened because they weren't listening while Horse was talking. Your horse is constantly talking to you, and as his protector and caregiver you owe it to him to learn to hear and understand everything he says. If your best friend or a family member began to moan and groan, limp around or just seemed uncomfortable in general, regardless of whether or not they verbalized a complaint, would you ignore the signs or would you take the time to try and figure out what the problem was? If you want your horse to be your friend and your companion, then treat him with the same courtesy and respect as you do your friends and family. If you will go beyond listening to hearing and understanding you will continue to have a safe and happy relationship with your magnificent companion.

My good friend Mark Schrimpf, owner of Bar S Quarter Horses located in Denton, Texas, is an excellent horseman and raises some of the finest performance horses in this country. I have had the pleasure of working with Mark for a number of years now and I know him to be an expert judge of horse character. He called me recently to discuss a two-year-old stud he was having a problem with.

He explained that he just could not seem to find a way to connect with this colt mentally. Mark knows and uses my technique to start all of his two-year-olds and he has had tremendous success with it. This colt was trying to tell him something and Mark knew it, but he was unable to determine what

Jay carrying pretty little Bailey at home on the farm in Oklahoma. *Photo courtesy of Carrie English.*

it was. Rather than push the colt harder and risk injury to the colt, the rider, or both, Mark backed off and tried a different approach. Because he is comfortable with his own talents and capabilities as a horseman, he wasn't ashamed to admit he did not have a solution to the problem and he sought my help.

I was not able to immediately offer a solution over the phone, but I went to Texas shortly thereafter to do a clinic. While I was there I paid a visit to Bar S Quarter Horses. Mark introduced me to this two-year-old and we got acquainted. He was a really nice-looking, well-built colt with a good conformation, but he was a bit smaller than the other colts his age. I watched him run around the arena by himself and I watched him in the pasture with the other horses. I watched Mark handle him and I watched Mark's trainer, Bill, work with him. Through my observation of the colt in these different settings, I came to the conclusion that the colt was scared to death.

Alone in the arena he was terrified and looking for someone to be his friend and protector. Mark and Bill both stand well over six feet tall and they were not only above him when they sat on his back, but when they stood next to him as well. His natural fear of things up above caused him to panic to the point that he was unable to stay around long enough to realize they were his friends. They were never not above him. Out in the pasture this was the colt that was cowering over in the corner because most of the other horses were bigger than he was. He was definitely at the bottom of the pecking order and the other big boys picked on him mercilessly.

I started working with him and taking things slow and easy to build his confidence. I stand about five feet seven inches tall so my presentation to him was a little less intimidating. When he first realized that he was big enough and brave enough to run my dog out of his barn lot he was quite proud of himself. My wife, Lane, stands five feet tall and she and Little Bit get along splendidly. She has taken over a lot of his care and handling since we brought him back to Tennessee with us so we could structure a training program specifically designed for him. He is no longer a stud but he is turning out to be one heck of a fine gelding, which is the norm for any horse that comes from the Bar S. Little Bit gets to travel with us since part of his training includes as much exposure to new sights and sounds as possible to help him overcome his fear and learn to be patient. We are not sure exactly where we are going with his training or what his final destination will be, but we are all enjoying our journey together.

Incidentally, the ten-year-old gelding, Jay, with the torn muscle in his side needed about three years of rest for the muscle to completely heal and to forget about the trauma he had endured. He now proudly carries a pretty little girl in rodeo grand entries back in Oklahoma. Sassy is still with her owners in Alabama. She slowly continues to improve physically but her mental recovery will take a bit longer because she was in so much pain for so long. Her owners are diligently working to learn how to communicate with her so that if she ever has something important to say again, they will know how to listen sooner.

I would like to see a better quality of life for all horses, especially those who are currently in the care of us humans. If I work with only the horses, then their quality of life is improved only while I am present. But if I can teach you how to communicate with your horses and understand the language of the horse, then every horse you have the privilege to work with during your lifetime has that same chance for a better life. If I give you a fish to eat you can eat one meal, but if I teach you how to fish then you can eat many meals. Learning to speak the language of the horse is but one step in the right direction. It is a small step, but by far the most important one.

Respect and Trust
Laying the Relationship Foundation

I grew up on my grandparents' farm near Bartlesville in northeast Oklahoma. Here was a land that consisted of large cattle ranches, small towns packed with pickup trucks on Saturday night, and mamas who couldn't stop their babies from growing up to be cowboys. I caught the fever early, perhaps having inherited it from my father, and it burned up my childhood days.

I was a terrible kid, always into something. I was hot-headed and would fight at the drop of a hat. I'd fight a buzz saw if one challenged me. I had no interest in school or anything else; I just wanted to be a cowboy. By the time I was twenty years old I was a full-time cowboy and all that that entailed, including a catalog of broken bones that grew larger year after year.

By my early forties I had worked my way up to assistant manager of the horse division of a 128,000-acre ranch not far from Bartlesville, where I worked from can to can't six days a week for almost twenty years. I have never lost my passion for the cowboy ways, but fortysomething is a time when men take stock of their lives, weigh their successes and failures, confront their own limitations, sense their own mortality, and adjust their attitudes.

I had broken just about every bone in my body, some more than once. I had seen a lot of cowboys and horses injured or permanently crippled by the methods we were using and I knew I was getting too old for that. Out of curiosity and physical necessity, I began to wonder if there might be a better way.

RESPECT AND TRUST WITHIN THE HERD

The lessons my father had tried to teach me still eluded me, but I began to recall the horses I had observed in the wild. I thought about the dominant mare whose position of authority was dependent upon two things: respect and trust. She commanded the respect of the other members of the herd by standing firm against challenges and she earned their trust by remaining alert for predators while the others slept or grazed. Their submission to her had nothing to do with fear.

I had learned about horses by watching them. They taught me about their pecking order, how they respect the boss mare, and how their places in the social circle are determined. I learned how they communicate and to appreciate their means of communication. The most important thing the horses had taught me was that they really are incredibly intelligent. Horses have minds. What I had to do was let them teach me how to work with theirs by using my own.

RESPECT, TRUST, AND DOMINANCE

Whether you are teaching a colt to halter or be saddled for the first time or working with the older, already-schooled horse, it is necessary for you to establish a pecking order with that horse. Horses are born with an instinctive understanding of this principle. You should be number one; he should be number two. You do not need to use force or fear to prove to a horse that you are tougher than he is. There is no need to lay a hand on him or whip him to gain social respect, because horses don't do that out in the pasture or in the wild. They do it with their body language. Gentle dominance and the way you handle the horse will command him to respect you in a way he understands.

The majority of the problems people encounter with their horses are due to a lack of these two things: respect and trust. Usually the lack is on the part of both parties involved, the horse and the rider. When you are working with your horse, regardless of his age or level of training, you need to have his respect first. If he doesn't respect you, all of your hard work will mean nothing. Teaching a horse this lesson in respect must begin on the ground, because if he doesn't have respect for you on the ground, he darn sure won't have any for you on his back. You're in a wreck that is looking for a place to happen. Riding a horse that has no respect for you, thinking that you'll fix whatever the problem is as you go along, is dangerous. It's like climbing to the top of a sixty-foot ladder that starts to shake and thinking you'll fix it by climbing down one rung instead of by going all the way back to the ground to make sure it is sitting on firm footing.

If your horse pushes on you, rubs all over you, nibbles on you, or otherwise comes into your space without being invited, he is not being affectionate, he's being disrespectful. He's dominating you. Watch horses out in a pasture and observe the methods they use to move each other around.

Your horse is doing the same thing to you because he has no respect for you. If your horse has not yet mastered Respect 101—that is, respect for you—he won't trust you either.

When you are out on a trail ride, if a bunch of other horses goes crashing past you and your horse wants to go with them, don't fault your horse. He thinks those other horses have seen danger somewhere and are running to save their lives. His very life may depend on it. Your horse wants to go with his buddies because he doesn't trust you. You have not convinced him that you can take care of him or protect him and keep him safe from the predators. You have not established yourself as the dominant member of the herd. If your horse can't trust you, then he won't respect you either. You can see how respect and trust go hand in hand and play a vital role in your relationship with your horse; in fact, they are the very foundation upon which that relationship must be built if it is to be successful.

Unfortunately, most people who want their horses to be happy and comfortable allow their horses to show blatant disrespect and never take any measures to correct the problems that follow. Then the problem snowballs and the horse gets a reputation as a "bad horse" because the owners can't handle him or someone gets hurt. Not long ago I was listening to a radio talk show host discuss parenting with a panel of experts. One of the experts, a psychologist, I think, had determined that one of the most prevalent problems with kids today is that mom and dad don't want to be parents, they want to be buddies with their kids. They never ask the kids to do anything or to take any responsibility for anything. Parents give the kids everything they ask for and ask nothing in return. The result is children who have little or no respect for authority. These kids often turn to violence as a means of dealing with anyone who tries to command their respect. I remember thinking that so it is in the world of horse training. Establish the rules and stick to them. Your horse will have a great deal of respect for you if you do. Once you start bending those rules, pretty soon your horse will forget what they were. He will also forget to respect you.

Recently, at the close of one of my Teaching by Asking seminars, a man and his wife approached me, introduced themselves, and proceeded to tell me all about a two-year-old filly they had raised. They said this little filly had never been any problem nor had she given them a moment's trouble. I congratulated them for having been fortunate enough to have a horse of that intelligence. They went on to tell me that they had even saddled her and climbed aboard. I asked them what happened and they replied, "Nothing. She didn't move when we saddled her and when we got on she just stood there." They walked away beaming like proud parents and I was thinking they probably had a world champion on their hands if they could find a horse show with a class that awarded blue ribbons for just standing there.

A few months later this same couple called me and asked if I would take this filly and work with her for a month or so. I was quite surprised, as they had originally described her as the perfect horse. When I asked them what the problem was, they explained that she had done fine when they saddled her and got on a few times but when they finally tried to get her to move, she exploded. She bucked the rider off, crashed into the barn wall, and tore up her new saddle. I told them to load her up and bring her to my barn where I could have a look at her. "No problem," they replied.

A week later these folks called and asked if I would come to their barn to have a look at the filly. They said they had tried to load her several times but were about as close to going to the moon for Christmas as they were to getting that horse in the trailer. I decided I had to meet this perfect little horse that had been "no trouble."

These people could not understand why their precious little filly had gone from Mary Poppins to more like Freddie Krueger. I explained to them that she had never given them any trouble because they had never asked her to do anything. I told them that up to this point everything had been more or less her idea or something she wanted to do. When they finally did ask her to do something that was not on her agenda, such as move her feet or get into the trailer, they got the equivalent of a spoiled child throwing a tem-per tantrum. They had not taken the time to teach her to respect or trust them and she blew up when they asked her to move and flatly refused to go into a trailer that frightened her.

I see this time after time, horse owners who never ask their horse to do anything he doesn't want to do. These horse owners have horses that walk on top of them, drag them around at the end of a lead rope, turn their rump to them in the stall, and never, ever allow themselves to be caught until they are darned good and ready to be caught. If a situation arises where an owner asks his horse to do something he doesn't want to do, because the horse has no respect for his owner, he throws his temper tantrum. More often than not the owner loses the fight, gets himself hurt, and his horse program comes to a screeching halt. The horse gets a bad reputation and may be sold along with his reputation, deserved or not, to someone else who is no more knowl-edgeable than the seller. If you look at horse's registration papers and he has had several owners in a relatively short period of time, be on the lookout for behavior problems, inexperienced owners, or both. The horse may be sent to a trainer who has a great understanding of the use of force and fear as training aids but has absolutely no knowledge of training foundations.

Many of the so-called problem horses I encounter are those who simply have no respect for their trainer because the trainer did not teach them respect first. All the other problems result from that. These horses have been allowed to establish themselves as the dominant ones in the herd and they are acting accordingly. Once they are taught a little respect, they usually cease to be problem horses. Teaching a horse to respect you is not done by force, fear, or abuse. Respect is taught by understanding the horse's instincts and asking for his respect in a language he understands. A basic knowledge of the horse's instincts and language are crucial elements. If you don't understand his instincts, you will not know that the horse doesn't respect you, and if you don't understand his language, you will not know when he has gained respect.

You can command respect without being abusive. Good parents command respect from their children without beating them. Successful employers command the respect of their employees without abuse, harassment, or threats. You can be firm in your relationship with your horse without being harsh or mean. I never had any respect for anyone who beat me; I only feared them. I may have submitted to those who beat me and so will your horse, but his submission to you will always be out of fear and never out of respect. On the other hand, I have the utmost respect for anyone who can show me a better way to do something without trying to make me feel stupid. I don't want someone using their position of authority to force me to do things their way. Those who reward my smallest efforts are the ones who make me want to try harder. It's the same with your horse. He will respond to force but he won't learn respect or trust. Force teaches him only one thing—fear. The first time you get into a tight situation with a horse that only knows fear, you'll be on your own. Your horse will be concentrating on saving his own life and he may put your life in danger in an effort to achieve his goal.

The key to handling most horses is to gain their trust. If a horse knows you aren't going to hurt him, he will cooperate and try to do what you ask him. The horse is often instinctively afraid of new situations, but by helping him face his fear and work through it, he will come to trust you. He will quickly learn you aren't going to hurt him or cause him to hurt himself. Never put him in a bind from which he has no escape or can find no relief such as tying him to a snubbing post and flailing at him with a blanket to "sack him out." It is also not wise to make him accept having his feet picked up by tying up his foot. I never force a horse to accept anything. I ask him.

THE RESPONSIBILITIES OF BEING DOMINANT

My goal is to teach the horse that his life is better wherever I am. I want him to know that things are quiet and comfortable for him and that he is safe when he is with me. Once I teach the horse this, I have to do everything in my power to make certain I have not lied to him. It will not take many lies on my part to destroy the trust my horse has in me as the dominant member of the herd and his protector. Once his trust has been destroyed, if a situation arises that makes the horse feel threatened in any way, he will revert back to his instinct to save his own life the only way he knows how, by fleeing if possible or fighting if not. In this situation he won't have much concern for where I am or how well I can ride because he no longer trusts me to protect him and keep him safe.

For many years I refused to work with other people's horses because I did not know how to bridge the communication gap between the horse and his owner. It seemed absurd for me to take in a horse and spend two hours, two days, two months, or however long it took to teach him to respect and trust me, only to send him back to an owner who could not communicate with him in a way he could understand. My heart hung heavy each time I sent a horse home to an owner, or had an owner send the horse to a trainer who beat on him, pulled on his face, or used some other method of force or fear to make him do what they wanted him to do.

My clinic horse, Bar S Fairly Dry, affectionately known as Rooster, is a prime example of a horse enduring a situation like this. Rooster is a five-year-old Quarter Horse gelding that comes from Bar S Quarter Horses. He is out of a Dry Doc and Gay Bar King mare that was bred to Mark Schrimpf's stallion, Fairhill Enterprise. I started Rooster under saddle as a two-year-old in Alton, Illinois, which is where the Bar S was located at the time. He was just about the finest horse I'd had the opportunity to work with. He was soft, gentle, and remarkably intelligent. He was an excellent futurity prospect and he was sent to a reining horse trainer in Texas, where his training program proceeded to go sour.

Though Rooster is a top-quality horse, regrettably it turned out that the trainer was not able to structure his program to fit Rooster's individuality. It is not known just exactly what happened to Rooster at the hands of this trainer, but it is certain that he endured harsh physical and mental training methods that he did not tolerate well. As a result, his chance to go to the three-year-old futurity fell by the wayside. When Mark found out what had happened to Rooster, he went to Texas and brought him home.

In 1996, Bar S Quarter Horses moved to Denton, Texas, and Mark called and asked me if I would come out and help him start his two-year-old colts. I saw Rooster again and Mark filled me in on all that had happened to him. I had the opportunity to get reacquainted with him and Rooster and I became great friends. Before I left Texas, Mark had made arrangements for me to own this fine gelding.

I spent a year just going slow with him and teaching him to trust me. He knows now without a doubt that I will do nothing to cause him harm. I have taught him to respect me as the one in charge, and out of that his trust in me has grown. If we are trail riding and all the other horses run off and leave

Sam Powell and his clinic horse, Bar S Fairly Dry (Rooster).

us in a cloud of dust, Rooster barely raises his head unless I give him a reason. He would rather be with me than with the other horses because he trusts me with his life. For that reason I make sure his life is good.

I learned from this situation that if I work with people and teach them to work with and communicate with their horses, I have a greater chance of improving the quality of life for horses everywhere. If I keep the lessons simple enough the people have a greater chance of understanding things from the horse's point of view.

Sam puts Rooster through some of his paces during a clinic demonstration.

FIRMNESS AND CONSISTENCY

To teach your horse the lesson in respect and trust you must have an understanding of his language, his instincts, and how to use them to your advantage. When a horse turns his rump to me, I don't strike him. I may clap my hands, kick dirt at his feet, or make a lot of noise. I'll do something to make him uncomfortable and let him know that what he is doing is unacceptable to me. This is the very first step in working with any horse. Command his respect. Establish yourself as the dominant member of the herd. He shows his respect for you by moving his rump out of your face, staying out of your space, and being polite. Moving his rump out of your face is a respect issue to him, but it is also a safety issue for you. I have never been kicked by a horse that was looking at me, and a horse that is looking at me is not running away from me. Besides, there is no place on the back end to put a halter, so why would you want it in your face?

If your horse is running around with his neck bowed, his ears pinned back, or his mouth tightly clamped shut, he's not being cute, he's being disrespectful. He is telling you to get out of his space. Never reward him for such behavior. Take note of his attitude before you dump his feed, give him a rub on the neck, or a treat of any kind. Humans often contribute to a horse's bad manners or unacceptable behavior because we fail to notice these things or we fail to recognize the fact that these things mean something to the horse. When you feed a horse, rub him, or treat him while his ears are pinned, his rump is in your face, or while he is doing anything else that should be considered unacceptable behavior, you have just rewarded him for that behavior. In the horse's mind that must have been what you wanted him to do and he will continue to do it.

The solution for these behaviors is not to strike the horse. It is simple: Don't dump the feed, don't rub his neck, and don't give him the treat until he acts in a more acceptable manner. Clap your hands, stomp your feet, or just turn around and leave, but don't ignore his behavior. Command his respect at all times, even when you are in a hurry. If it is wrong for him to turn his rump to you today, then it must also be wrong for him to do it tomorrow, next week, next month, and next year. You must be consistent with your teaching if you expect him to be consistent with his learning. If you become sloppy or impatient, then he will learn bad habits. If you bend the rules he will forget there ever were any. Most often the problem horses I see are horses with bad manners, and bad manners can be attributed to lack of respect.

If you don't mind your horse walking on top of you, refusing to get in the trailer, go in the barn, or stand tied, then you probably don't see you have a problem. Once a lady told me that her horse would not cross water. However, she did not see that as a problem. She just never rode anywhere there was water. Many years ago I had an old pickup truck I decided to sell. That truck had never given me any problem because I knew the transmission was bad and had no reverse. I just never took it anywhere that I had to back it out of, so for me there was no problem. Its new owner did not quite see it that way when he drove it into the garage that night. He definitely saw a problem when he asked it to back out the next morning. It just goes to show that problems are like beauty, all in the eye of the beholder.

I would be almost willing to bet that you would not allow your best friend to walk on you, get in your face, push around on you, bite you, or otherwise invade your space, so why would you allow your horse to do it? If your friend were to behave in such a manner, chances are you would waste no time in letting him know that his behavior was disrespectful and unacceptable. While it might be dangerous for your friend to do these things to you, it is much more dangerous for you if you allow your horse to do them to you.

Being firm in your relationship with your horse and commanding his respect has nothing to do with being abusive, harsh, or mean. The horse's mother was firm with him and occasionally she disciplined him for misbehaving. In your relationship with your horse, disciplinary action may be called for, such as in the case of a horse that bites. Biting is not only a sign of blatant disrespect—it is extremely dangerous and should be corrected immediately.

When a horse bites or even nibbles at you and you allow him to do it, in his mind he has dominated you and from that point on he will not have much respect for you. He should be disciplined for the action while he is in the process of the action. A horse thinks in milliseconds, and whatever discipline you use must be applied at the exact moment the infraction occurs, because he will associate what you do to him with whatever he is doing at that precise moment. If your horse bites you and you pull your arm away, go crying into the house to get the peroxide and a Band-Aid, and then return to the barn and proceed to work him over with a two-by-four, he will have no idea why you are doing that to him. In his mind you have beaten him for doing nothing but standing there. On the other hand, if the disciplinary action occurs while he is coming towards you to bite, or while his mouth is still on you, he knows exactly why you disciplined him. However, it means nothing if he is in the process of moving away from biting. The amount of time it takes a fly to buzz by is about the length of the horse's attention span.

TIMING OF DISCIPLINE

Whatever form of discipline you use at the time, use it only once. Once is discipline, twice is abuse. A horse respects his mother for her intolerance of his disrespect and he will respect you in the same manner. A disrespectful horse can cause injury and even death if you allow him to get away with it. He will fear you if you abuse him and he may hurt you if you allow him to be disrespectful. There is a delicate balance here, but never, ever think that you need to make your horse afraid of you to make him respect you. Familiarize yourself with the means by which horses show disrespect and dominance by observing them yourself. I chose biting as an example because it is so vicious and dangerous.

You would be amazed at how quickly a horse can remove a finger carelessly placed near his mouth. A friend of mine was picked up by the shoulder and carried out across the pasture while being shaken like a rag doll by a horse. The result of a split second of carelessness on the part of my friend was that I got to be a pallbearer at his funeral. I am conveying this information to you not to make you afraid of horses, but to help you respect their potential and understand their point of view.

If you will try to understand what is going on in the horse's mind, then you will know why he reacts the way he does. If you approach your horse with a new understanding and tolerance that is based on mutual respect, trust, and patience, your horse will respond to you in ways you never thought possible.

All of the horses I work with go through the lesson in respect and trust first. Regardless of age, level of training, breed, or color, they have to learn respect for the dominant member of the herd—me. This lesson tells me a lot about where the horse's mind is so I am better able to assess how much mental pressure he can handle. If a horse is brought to me because of a specific behavioral problem that is rooted in a lack of respect, then I can eliminate the problem and its cause in one lesson. The horse may or may not respect his owner, but if I am to be his teacher, I must have his respect.

The respect I teach the horse to have for me is not transferable. I can't teach the horse to respect his owner—the owner will have to do that—but I can teach the owner how to gain that respect before he leaves with his horse. If you will teach your horse to respect you before you teach him anything else, he will be more willing to learn the other lessons. If you then teach him to trust you, he will do his best to try to do whatever you ask of him.

TEACHING RESPECT AND TRUST

The lessons in respect and trust go hand in hand and begin in a sixty-foot diameter, open-sided round pen. Use a sixty-footer because all horses have an imaginary safety bubble that extends out about twenty-five to thirty feet around them. Have you ever noticed that when you go out to catch your horse and he doesn't want to be caught, he will allow you to get about twenty-five or thirty feet from him before walking off a little ways? Then he stops and goes back to grazing and allows you to get about twenty-five or thirty feet from him again, when he takes a few more steps away and once more starts grazing. That is his safety zone. If he can maintain this distance, chances are he will probably be able to escape if the situation becomes critical and he perceives danger or hostility. If he allows you to get any closer, then his chances of escape are diminished.

In a sixty-foot round pen, you can stand in the center and be thirty feet away, out of the horse's safety zone. Take one step out of the center in any direction and you will put mental pressure on the horse, or step back to the center, take the pressure off, and allow him to calm down and think. Horses learn not by applying pressure but by taking it off at the right moment. People who tell me that they tried working with their horse in a round pen but couldn't keep him from trying to jump out of it generally admit they were using a pen that was forty-five feet or smaller in diameter. You can't get out of the horse's safety zone in a pen of this size. He can never find relief from the mental pressure. His reward for doing the right thing and his motivation to keep doing it the right way has to be relief from the mental pressure you are putting on him. You must have a pen large enough to allow you to do that. However, using a round pen that is larger than sixty feet will cause you to work yourself to death trying to keep pressure on the horse

I put the horse in the round pen and allow him to move freely around it. Horse owned by Julia Brown.

long enough to get a response. He won't learn a darned thing except that he can tire you out long before you can tire him out.

I used to use a solid-sided round pen. I was the only thing there for the horse to pay attention to so he had no choice but to pay attention. But sooner or later you will have to ride him outside where there are dogs barking, kids on their bicycles, and mailmen who honk their horns and wave. The horse might as well get used to these things sooner rather than later, and he can get better exposure to them in an open-sided round pen. You want to know the horse's attention is on you because that is the best place for it to be, not because that is the only place. You want your horse to make that choice. Exposing your horse to such distractions in the beginning may improve your social life as well. You won't have to deal with neighbors who think you are rude when you ride past their house without waving because you are holding on to your horse for dear life.

Start a horse in an open-sided round pen. The only difference between the inside of that pen and the outside world with all of its distractions is the half-inch board or the inch-and-one-quarter pipe with which the pen is constructed. If you can get him to mentally hook up with you despite the distractions, then you can be assured his attention is on you because he wants it there. You will find him much more receptive to what you are trying to teach him.

Put the horse in the round pen and allow him to run freely around it just as he would in the pasture. He will continue to run until he realizes that you are not going to hurt him. He has no idea of what is right or wrong at this

When the horse relaxes and accepts my presence in the pen, I let him stop. If he looks at me I allow him to stand there and catch his breath.

point, so it is up to you to teach him. Just keep showing him what it is you want him to do.

The first few minutes you spend with a colt in the beginning stages is very important. I always want my horses to have a good first impression. If his first impression is good, it is easier to build the relationship from that point. Show a horse that you will not harm him. Allow him to learn at his own speed.

As the horse moves around the round pen, not much seems to be happening to the untrained eye, but in reality, you are in control of the horse. If he turns his rear end to you even a little bit, send him away. Then make him move his rear end around toward the fence. To get him to move around the pen, stand at his hip just out of the center of the round pen and encourage him to move out by making him uncomfortable with smooching sounds or by waving your arms. To stop him, block his forward motion by stepping toward his shoulder. By using this back and forth movement you can move the horse where you want him on the rail.

While he is working, pay attention to his gauges. His eyes, his ears, his mouth, and the way he carries his head will tell you if he is frightened, timid, or aggressive or whether he is starting to relax and pay attention. (Go back to Chapter Two for a quick review in order to understand what your horse might be telling you.)

When the horse relaxes and accepts your presence in the pen, let him stop. If he looks at you, let him stand there, catch his breath, and think the situation over a little bit. When he is allowed to catch his breath, he starts to feel good about stopping and he begins to realize that he doesn't have to keep working. At this point, start to approach him. If he turns his rump or runs away, continue to work him in the pen. Drive him away from you and get him to work a bit more, maybe a bit faster. Then allow him to stop again. As you approach him, watch for signs of fear. If he starts looking for an escape, stop your approach, take the mental pressure off and let him relax for a minute and then move closer. When you are close enough to touch him, stop short of doing so; turn your back to him and walk away.

When ready to establish contact, approach the horse just slightly from the side, with arm outstretched and palm turned down. Allow him to approach you at his own speed. Give him the opportunity to check you out; don't just run over and grab his hand and start shaking it. Once he lets you approach and you make successful contact by sniffing your hand, if you think he can handle the pressure, stroke him on the side of his face or on his neck. If he indicates that he can't deal with this, turn and walk away, thus removing the mental pressure.

Sending a horse around the pen puts him in a mental bind, but walking away from him does two things. It tells him you are not going to hurt him and it establishes you at the top of the pecking order. You have told him it is not acceptable for him to turn his rump to you but you have turned yours to him. You have begun to establish respect as the dominant member of the herd.

When you can walk to his hip and have him move it over and continue to face you, then you have his respect. Anytime he stops and faces you, reward him by rubbing or stroking his neck or along the top of his mane. Do something that is pleasant to him to let him know that was the right

When I am ready to establish contact I approach the horse with my palm turned down and allow the horse to get to know me at his own pace.

When I can walk to his hip and have the horse move it over and continue to face me, I know I have his respect.

move. Anything you can do that mimics the way horses treat one another is helpful in most cases. They don't usually pat each other and this can sometimes be frightening to a young horse not accustomed to being handled. Once a horse looks at you consistently, slowly ease toward his hip. At this point he has a choice. He can either run or he can move his hip over. If he runs, then we go back to work around the pen and he knows that was the wrong thing because now he is not comfortable. Allow him to stop and face you and again move toward his hip. If he makes even a tiny effort to move his hip away from you, reward him. Always reward the slightest effort even if it is only a shifting of his weight in the right direction. When he will move his hip over consistently each time you approach, you have his respect. He will keep his rump out of your face because he knows you will send him to his room if he does not.

Consistently reward the horse for the efforts he makes. He will begin to understand that things are quieter and more pleasant for him wherever you are. When you walk away from him and he follows, he is starting to trust. Horses will often follow you around out of simple curiosity, but that has nothing to do with trust. The only way you can convince a horse to trust you is to first teach him to respect you. It just won't work any other way.

When I can walk away and he follows, he is starting to trust me.

AFTER THE FIRST LESSONS

Throughout the rest of the horse's training program, you should continue to build on the foundation started in the round pen. If you will continue to respect him enough to present all aspects of your training program to him in a manner he can understand, he will continue to respect you and trust that you are not going to hurt him. You will then find in your horse a much more willing student.

Because respect and trust go hand in hand, it is difficult, if not impossible, to have one without the other. Remember that in the wild, once the dominant mare has the respect of the other members of the herd they instinctively trust her to keep them safe. Her dominance of the others is based on their respect of her, not on fear. Before you command the respect of your horse be certain you are worthy of it and will be able to fulfill the responsibilities that go along with it. Once you teach a horse to trust you to make his life better, make sure it is better. Respect and trust must be the basis for all your relationships, human or animal. These qualities may not be everything, but without them you have little to work with. Basing a training program or a relationship on anything else is like constructing your house on a weak or faulty foundation. No matter how well that house is constructed, without a solid foundation, it will crumble to the ground when things get rough.

Teaching and Training
Understanding the Basics

In a lifetime of working on ranches in Oklahoma, Texas, Arizona, and Tennessee, I learned to break and train horses using the traditional methods. We saddled the horses, blindfolded them, prodded them with sharp spurs while directing them with a harsh bit and a leather lash, and bucked them into exhaustion. That was part of the cowboy image and mentality. You had to be tough to do the work and you were constantly trying to assert your toughness.

The longer I worked with horses with this tough-guy, macho-man attitude the more bones the horses broke and the more crippled I became. The more crippled I became, the more I realized that I was at a serious disadvantage in my negotiations with these creatures. A 150-pound man can't inflict enough pain on a 1,200-pound animal to make it behave the way he wants. I might eventually conquer him but it was going to mean a trip or two to the hospital for one or both of us.

STARTING VERSUS BREAKING

After suffering more broken bones than I want to remember and seeing a sad number of other cowboys and horses crippled by the methods we were using, I started to re-evaluate. I began to withdraw into myself and try to figure a way to get into the horse's mind and convince him I had a better idea. I read everything I could get my hands on about training horses and the more I read, the more I was convinced I could not train a horse.

I wanted to stop breaking horses and find a way to bring them around to my way of thinking without causing injury to either of us. Instead of trying to train a horse to act contrary to his own genetic instruction book, why couldn't I play on his instincts to establish a relationship in which we both

My father did not handle horses like other cowboys I had known. He was patient, soft-spoken, and cajoling. Horse owned by Del Powell. *Photographer unknown.*

got what we wanted? I put the pieces of the puzzle together differently than I had before and developed a method of working with horses that has since taken me around the world to teach other horse people.

As I began to reconstruct the pieces of the puzzle, I started recalling the lessons my father had tried to teach me about horses, animal nature, and human nature. Something he had done many years before came back to me, but it had nothing to do with horses. He was standing by the barn holding up a piece of wood, and he remarked rather casually and to no one in particular, "If I had a hammer, I'd nail this board up." I went running off to get that hammer for him as fast as I could. Now, if he had told me to go get the hammer I am sure I would have rebelled, thrown a fit, and thought of a thousand and one reasons not to go and get it. But Dad let me think that going after that hammer was all my idea and I did it not only willingly but with great pride and enthusiasm.

My father did not handle horses like the other cowboys I had known. He was patient, soft-spoken and cajoling. "You can't whip horses into shape," he told me. He seemed to talk rather than force the horses into submission, which grated on me in my younger days. I thought he was doing it that way because he was an old man; after all that wasn't the way the real, macho cowboys did it.

Many years ago men like my father were called "horse whisperers" and were thought to possess supernatural ways with animals. They were contrarians who preferred to gentle rather than break horses. They knew the horse's true nature, his mind, instincts, likes, dislikes, temperament, and the behavior that had been bred into the horse for eons. Their methods were not embraced for economic and cultural reasons. On large ranches where dozens, perhaps hundreds, of horses have to be trained in a single season a quick rodeo was preferred to the slow moving ways of these eccentric equestrians.

The rugged cowboy culture had always held to sterner methods. Horses were broken—with all that the term implied. Until my forties, I too clung to the old ways. Physical necessity and curiosity led me to utilize horse training techniques that have placed me, along with a handful of others, at the forefront of a widening movement that is causing cowboys, ranchers, horse owners and weekend riders to reconsider their relationships with horses.

There is nothing mystical about it. There's no voodoo involved. It isn't complicated—you only have to understand the horse's mind and work with it instead of against it. I have found that most horses, however fearful or belligerent their attitude, can be approached, saddled and ridden without the rodeo style toughness usually associated with domesticating a horse that is unaccustomed to human contact. The technique has worked on horses brought to my clinics from rodeo bucking strings by those hoping to discredit me.

I teach patience and communication. The lessons I teach in the round pen can even be applied to human lives and should be learned by everyone. I don't use the term breaking horses. I refer to what I do as starting them. I communicate with the horse so he understands what I want him to do. Once he understands what it is I want from him, I have to be patient enough to give him time to learn how to do it.

Every time you ask your horse to do something new, give him time to figure it out on his own. He will learn more quickly if you will allow him to make mistakes and simply reward him for effort in the right direction. He will try harder and respect you more if you allow him to figure it out for himself. Don't punish him for doing things wrong; reward him for doing them right.

TEACHING BASICS

Working with horses has taught me a lot about working with people. I have two daughters. I wish I had been smart enough when they were growing up to do with them what I do with the horses—give them a chance to learn. They wanted to do things one way, as all kids do, while I wanted to do them another, as all parents do. I lacked the patience and knowledge to set things up for them and give them the latitude to learn for themselves. Horses and people learn by making mistakes, trying again, and being rewarded for doing the right thing, not by being beaten or forced.

Children are not born knowing how to walk, so when they begin to learn they fall a lot. What a sad world this would be if parents beat or threatened children every time they fell down. Most parents are patient and encouraging with a child no matter how long it takes for him to make that first successful step. Soon the child is able to take more and more steps without falling down and, once he masters walking, running generally comes with ease. However, I have never seen a person run who has not first learned to walk. If we humans have enough patience to wait the weeks or months it takes for our children to learn to walk, why is it that we often expect our horses to learn everything they will ever have to know in thirty days or less? Why is it that we seem to expect them to know how to run before they can walk?

Our children, as a rule, attend school for a period of twelve years. During the first six years they learn the same basics, each year becoming a little more advanced. During the second six years half of the classes are a little more specialized, but the other half are still only more advanced versions of the basics they began learning in grades one though six. Advancement into the next grade or to the next level should be based on successful completion or mastering of the previous one. If a student cannot successfully add and subtract or has difficulty grasping the concept, then advancement to multiplication and division will be a frustrating and difficult time for him. He may be fortunate enough to slide by only to discover he can't get through fractions, or algebra, geometry or trigonometry. At some point the student will hit that proverbial brick wall and his math program will fall apart because it was not build on a solid foundation of the basics.

Once the student successfully completes this aspect of his education, he begins to decide the direction he wants to go with his life and goes into a training program geared toward that ultimate goal. If he wants to be a doctor, he goes to medical school. If he wants to be an electrician, he becomes an electrical apprentice, and so on. Regardless of the specialty line of work the student decides to go into, training for that specific line of work can only begin after he has learned the basics. The success of the training program will depend upon how well and how thoroughly the basics have been mastered.

Working with your horse is no different. Without adequate training in the basics he will never live up to his full training potential. He needs a solid foundation upon which the rest of his training program can be built. There are three basics that constitute the beginning of the foundation I put on all my horses. I want my horse soft in the poll, or to give me his face vertically. I want him soft from side to side, or to give me his face laterally, and I want him to move away from pressure applied with my leg, or to move off my leg. I spend as much time as it takes to teach him to do these three things and we don't go to Lesson Two until Lesson One is complete, correct and solid. I teach these three basics using the principle of what I call the three R's.

THE THREE R'S

The three R's represent request, response, and release. When you ask your horse to do something, that is a request. Depending upon what you are asking him to do, you usually ask by applying physical pressure somewhere on his body or mental pressure to his brain. When your horse does what you ask him to and does it correctly, that is the response you are looking for. If he responds correctly to your request, his reward is the immediate and complete release from the pressure.

Whether you are teaching him to move his body over, position his head, back up, or anything else, applying the pressure is not what teaches him. The moment when you release the pressure is when he learns what you want. If you hold the pressure until he gets it right and then release, he will go back to the point at which he found relief from the pressure.

When I talk about applying pressure, I am not talking about using a come-along to pull his face around or a concrete block weight to get his head down. I mean starting out with the least amount of pressure needed to get a response. If it takes two ounces of pressure, then why would you want to do the extra work it takes to apply seven ounces? On the other hand, if it takes seven, then two won't do much good. The amount of pressure you need to apply is only the amount needed to get a response. Releasing the pressure is the horse's motivation for a correct response, provided the release comes only when the response is correct. If you release the pressure when he is doing the wrong thing, then he thinks that is what you want. If he gives you a correct response and you do not release the pressure, he becomes confused about what you are asking.

In the beginning a horse's progress must be measured in millimeters. Reward him for even a thought in the right direction. If you are attempting to teach him to back up on cue, apply the pressure and then reward him for just shifting his weight backwards. He doesn't know anything about what you are asking him to do and he has to have time to figure it out. If you want him to get it right the next time, you will have to let him know he did it right the first time.

Everything you do with a horse prepares him for a transition to the next step. Each step builds on the previous one, provided it was successfully completed. You can look up at the top of a sixty-foot ladder while standing on the ground, but the only way to get to there is by going up one rung at a time. Don't move to the next step with your horse until the previous step is complete, correct, and solid. People often tell me that their horses will do really well at a walk or a trot but want to run off with them at a lope. This is a prime example of a program that was not built on a solid foundation. If you have no control of the horse at a lope then you don't have solid control at the walk or trot either. Go back and spend more time learning how to drive slowly before you press on the accelerator.

I start teaching my colts the alphabet from A to Z. The fundamentals begin with things such as a walk, trot, lope, turn around, and back up. I make sure he knows A before we progress to B. Thus, I never have to go back to A again. Once the horse knows the alphabet, he is ready to progress to more extensive specialized training.

YOUR HORSE'S PROGRESS

Always remember to go at a pace your horse can relate to and tolerate. You will not be able to teach him about physical pressure if he can't handle the mental pressure you are putting on him. Most people go too fast in teaching their horses. They want to progress from day care to college in one day. Moving too quickly is detrimental to the horse's ability to retain the information. If you pour water rapidly into a bucket, more of it winds up splashing out on the ground than going in the bucket. Try thinking of your horse's brain as the bucket and what you are trying to teach him as the water.

Never decide in advance how long it will take to teach your horse to do something. Don't set a time limit on him. If it takes him thirty minutes or thirty days to learn to do one thing really well, then be consistent enough with your teaching and patient enough with your asking for him to learn it. Putting a time limit on him jeopardizes the longevity of his learning. If you put too much mental pressure on your horse, you won't accomplish anything in the long run. Allow him to learn at his own speed. Your horse has a brain and he will use it if you allow him. The first thing I tell people at my Teaching by Asking Clinics is that, when working with horses, you should throw away your clocks and calendars because horses can't read either one of them. Horses have no concept of time, and they have the attention span of a Bartlett pear.

You can start teaching your horse at a relatively young age, but sending him to school before he is ready is like trying to fit a square peg into a round hole. You'll both be frustrated, but ultimately the one to suffer will be the horse. Different horses have different learning capabilities. They do not all mature mentally or physically at the same rate. One horse may be ready to start school before he is two years old while another may not be mentally ready until well past his second birthday, despite the fact that he stands over sixteen hands high and weighs 1,200 pounds.

On the ranch in Oklahoma, we normally started our colts in the spring of their second year. By futurity time the next fall we had some idea of which ones would fit our program and which ones would not. There was one particular horse that had matured very well physically. He was a well-built, stout, good-looking stallion, but when I got ready to start him under saddle he just was not as mentally mature as I needed him to be. He preferred to watch butterflies or chase birds around the paddock. His attention span was practically nonexistent. He would watch me for a second or two, but was too easily distracted. He left me a couple of times and went to the other side of the pen to watch dogs walking by. So, I moved him to the end of the training line.

By September of his second year his mental maturation had caught up with his physical. Within an hour after I began working with him I could ride him outside the round pen. Unfortunately he was six months behind all the other colts in his training, which meant he was out of the three-year-old futurity, but his breeding made him a great candidate for cutting or reining. I worked with him for about six weeks and the ranch sent him to a reining horse trainer in Texas.

While he was at the trainer's, Mark Schrimpf from Bar S Quarter Horses happened by one day and saw him. Mark knew he liked him, but he was not in the market for a stallion. He wanted to own a son of Doc-O-Lena, but not at that particular time. Later he had the opportunity to have another look at the colt and watch him move. This colt was talented—not fast but he was calculating. Every move he made looked as though it had been carefully choreographed. Mark asked the owners to price the colt and went away the owner of Lena's Gyrator, an own son of Doc-O-Lena out of a daughter of Jewels Leo Bars (Freckles).

I had ridden Gyrator for a total of six weeks and he had been at the trainer's for another six weeks when Mark bought him. Three days after Mark purchased Gyrator in early February, the colt colicked and had to have surgery. He was out of training a total of eight weeks to recuperate. Once he was able to go back into training he had to be brought along slowly and

Lena's Gyrator, Open Division Champion 1993 National Reining Horse Association Super Stakes. Horse owned by Mark Schrimpf. *Photographer Waltenberry, Inc.*

reconditioned. Now he was about ten months behind in his official training schedule and all the other colts his age had passed by him.

As a three-year-old with a total of twenty weeks' training, Gyrator went to the Ak-Sar-Ben Open Reining competition where he scored 221 points. At the futurity later that year, with a total of only thirty weeks' training, he lost the finals on a judge's call. Gyrator went on to win the 1993 Open Lazy E Reining with a score of 226, and he was the Derby Reserve Champion by a half point. He also won the Super Stakes in Ohio and qualified for the AQHA World Show. He placed fifth in the 1993 World with a chipped bone in his leg. The bone chip was removed from his leg and he was retired. Lena's Gyrator has been standing at stud at Bar S Quarter Horses since then. At the time of this writing, Gyrator is being brought out of retirement and put into a conditioning program in an attempt to qualify for the United States Equestrian Team reining competition when it becomes part of the summer Olympics program.

Being behind in the beginning did not deter Gyrator from being able to catch up with his competition in the long run. He became a winner with about half as much training time as the other horses he was competing against. Allowing him to mature mentally before I ever started him helped him to overcome his physical setbacks and go on to surpass the competition. He became a true champion because he had the mind to do what was needed.

When I agree to take a horse to work with at my barn, the first thing the owners want to know is what I will have him doing at the end of thirty days. Often they seem a bit perplexed when I tell them that I don't know—it depends on the horse. Some horses grasp the basics in thirty days, while others take six months or more. One horse may tolerate a training session of forty-five minutes, while another may have all he can handle at the end of ten minutes. If you try to fit the horse with the ten-minute attention span into the forty-five minute training program he will become frustrated and confused. Your own frustration with his confusion will cause you to become impatient and intolerant of his mistakes at a time when patience and tolerance are the two most important things you can give him.

Frustration will cause the horse to become increasingly more difficult to handle because he can find no relief from the mental pressure you are putting on him to learn. He will probably develop bad habits such as bucking, fighting the bit, or running away. This results in you feeling that you have to use more severe equipment or harsher training methods. The whole situation then snowballs and can result in you or the horse getting injured or killed, whether by accident or on purpose.

At the end of thirty days one horse might just be walking really, really well while another one might be able to stick his butt in the ground and slide thirty feet to a stop. It all depends on the horse's mental and physical capabilities and how patient and tolerant you are while presenting the program to him.

WORKING WITH THE INDIVIDUAL HORSE

In 1994, as I was returning to my home in Tennessee from the west where I had been conducting clinics, I happened upon a gentleman who had tied his horse to a tree alongside the road and had proceeded to work him over with a two-by-four upside his head. I stopped to see if I might be able to offer some assistance to the horse. I asked the man what he was trying to do and he informed me that he was trying to kill the horse. I thought he was doing a pretty good job of it and asked him why. He told me he had bought this Thoroughbred from the racetrack with the intention of making a barrel horse out of him, but that the horse was so dumb he just kept running off. I knew the horse didn't have a chance with this owner. Why? Because Thoroughbreds who are to be used on the track are never, never, ever permitted to turn to the right. Every racetrack in the country is run with the

After I spent a year teaching Ridgerunner how to walk, I ponied other horses off him, roped off him and dragged brush off him. Horse owned by Leigh Ann Bratton.

Leigh Ann and Ridgerunner are great trail riding friends now. *Photo courtesy of Leigh Ann Bratton.*

turns to the left and the horse needs to be able to stay in his left-hand lead at all times. The split second it takes a horse to change leads could cost him a race, so he is never allowed to move in anything other than the left lead. If a racehorse's stall is on the right side of the barn his handler will lead him past that stall and around the block so he can make a left-hand turn to go in the stall. However, in a barrel race, depending on how you run the pattern, either the first or second turn the horse will make is a right-hand turn. He has to pick up or change to a right lead, and the racehorse won't know how to do it because of the intense deconditioning over a period of time. The horse gets scared and knocks the barrel over, or he falls down because his feet get tangled up, or he takes the bit and does the only thing he knows how to do—he runs away.

This horse had thrown a fit and knocked the barrel over because he did not know how to do what the rider was asking him. The rider did not know that, being a Thoroughbred racehorse, the horse had never been trained to turn right. All the rider knew was that the horse could run. I guess he just assumed the horse could figure the rest out on his own. This man's ignorance nearly cost the horse his life.

I offered a killer price for the horse. He agreed, so I paid a little over $400.00 for a horse I really did not need, but to stand there and watch him being mistreated or killed was out of the question. I brought Ridgerunner home and spent an entire year just teaching him how to walk. He already knew how to run—what he needed was to know that he didn't have to run anymore. We rode lots of trails in the hills of middle and East Tennessee. I roped off him, dragged brush off him, and ponied other horses off him. He turned out to be one of the best horses I have ever owned.

In 1996 I sold Ridgerunner to a lady close to my home in Tennessee. She fell in love with him and asked me to sell him. I have no regrets as the two of them are great friends and spend a lot of time trail riding together. She cares for him and has provided him with a good home. I get the opportunity to check on them, and occasionally she and Ridgerunner go trail riding with our group. What might have been a tragic end for a retired racehorse turned out to be a new and happier life for him.

THE IMPORTANCE OF FUNDAMENTALS

So many people make the mistake of just getting on a horse and riding him instead of taking the time to teach him the fundamentals. Without the fundamentals you have no control. It's like being at the top of a mountain in a car that has no brakes and no steering wheel. Without control, if your horse becomes frightened, you're in danger. People think that because they are not falling off, they are able to ride and there is no problem.

In the summer of 1997 I conducted a clinic for a local pony club. I agreed to do the clinic with some trepidation because of the "pony club" part. Past experience gave me the feeling that this probably would not be the best clinic I had ever done. It was to be a horsemanship clinic, and I arrived to find ten horses tacked up and ten riders of varying ages from eight to twelve years in helmets and flack jackets.

Shortly after we began I understood the necessity of the safety equipment the kids were wearing. Never in my life have I ever seen so many spoiled-rotten, dangerous horses in one place being ridden by children. I was appalled and certainly had my work cut out. When I taught the first horse his lesson in respect, to the credit of the children, they all wanted their horses to have that same lesson before we proceeded further with the horsemanship part of the clinic.

After the clinic was over, I took questions from the audience. Someone asked me what I thought about the care of the parents in having bought the children the best helmets and most expensive flack jackets available. I told them I thought the safety equipment was a good idea, especially with these horses, but if they really wanted to do something to keep their children safe, they might start with buying them better horses. Safety equipment can play a tremendous role if it is used wisely in conjunction with a well-trained, well-behaved horse—not instead of one. Depending on safety equipment to keep you from getting hurt on a horse when the problem is that the horse isn't broke or you don't know how to ride is like going up in an airplane you don't know how to fly just because you have a parachute strapped to your back.

In my experience over the years, show horses are the ones that are usually seriously lacking in the basics. Many are well-trained and go on to win a lot of money and blue ribbons, but they have not been taught the fundamentals they need in order to be what I consider good horses. Because they are kept stabled so much of the time, these horses are more sheltered and are exposed to fewer things to frighten them throughout the course of a normal day than a typical pleasure horse. These horses need the basics. When they are exposed to new things on the show circuit they tend to spook easily. You must have some means to help them control that fear. If a horse has not been taught to give you his face from side to side when you ask for it you will not be able to pull him around in a circle if he gets scared and tries to run off. If he has not learned to pick up his right foot when you pick up a right rein, then pulling his head around when he runs off with you will not work because he won't know what it means. Pulling his head around does not mean that his body will follow unless that was taught to him. The only thing on his mind will be saving his life. Regardless of your long-term plans for your horse, putting a solid foundation on him will help him show better in the long run and it could possibly save your life. There is no way to completely bombproof a horse, but you can do a lot to help him control his fear.

At one of my clinics I demonstrated my bombproof theory to the audience using a horse that had spooked from a rag that was tied to one of the panels of the round pen. Once I got him to face the rag and realize it was not going to hurt him, I moved the rag to the next panel. When the horse came around the pen and saw the rag again, he spooked. Again, I got him to face the rag and calm down. Then I moved the rag to the next panel and the horse spooked again. There were eighteen ten-foot panels constructing that round pen and I tied the same rag to every panel in it. Every time I moved the rag to another panel it spooked the horse because, even though it was the same rag, in the horse's mind it was different because it was in a different spot. Remember, we are trying to consider the horse's perception here, and he perceived that rag as something new and frightening each time I moved it to a new position on the fence.

A couple asked me to train the horse they bought for their daughter. She was twelve years old and had never ridden. Her parents went to a sale and purchased a two-year-old gelding that had not yet been started under saddle. They thought that their daughter and the horse could grow up together, plus they just could not afford the $3,000 for an older, well-broke horse. They wanted me to break the horse for their daughter to ride and guarantee that he would be bombproof when I sent him home. They offered to pay me in advance, which I told them would be fine. When they asked me how much they should make the check out for, I told them $6,000, explaining that my training fee was $500 per month and that it would be at least a year before I would even consider sending him back to a twelve-year-old who did not know how to ride. I asked them to also consider spending about another $2,000 for riding lessons for their daughter. I went on to tell them that I would not guarantee the horse would be bombproof no matter how long I kept him. The father did some figuring and, in a somewhat downtrodden tone of voice, told me that after a year with me his horse would be worth $6,800. I explained to him that, no, his horse would still only be worth $800, but that he would have $6,800 invested in him.

Tragically, a lovely lady recently experienced a severe head injury , multiple broken bones, a helicopter ride to the hospital, cardiac arrest, and months of intensive rehabilitation because of a horse with no control. The rider was not at fault; she was applying the brakes to an out-of-control race car that had no brakes. Nor was it the horse's fault that whomever had taught him how to go around an arena real nice forgot to teach him how to stop. You don't fault the race car because the mechanic forgot to install the brakes. You owe it to yourself to make sure your horse has brakes before you get in a situation where you need them, and you owe it to yourself to know where those brakes are and how to use them.

My intention is not to make people afraid of horses. On the contrary, I want people everywhere to know what wonderful creatures and companions horses are. My intention is to show you how foolish and dangerous it can be to train a horse before you teach him the basics. I want to emphasize how important it is for you to know the difference between teaching and training, and how vital it is for your safety or that of your horse that he understands the basics. Both of you need that solid foundation upon which to build specialized training. If you will keep the horse's survival instincts in mind as you are teaching him, you will be able to figure out why he sometimes reacts the way he does.

THE LARIAT AS A TEACHING AID

My method, Teaching by Asking, goes back to the core basics of horsemanship. All you need to successfully apply my teachings is common sense, a lot of patience, respect for the horse, and an understanding of the three R's. If you will learn the three R's, learn how to use them, and teach them to your horse, you will see amazing results.

Throughout the horse's life he will need to respond to pressure either from the bit in his mouth or from the rider's leg. He should be taught to respond to pressure early on, although moving away from pressure is not a natural thing for a horse. He can be taught to give to pressure, but the horse's natural instinct is to push back on anything that pushes on him.

In the wild, when predators begin their pursuit of the wild horses the horses' first instinct is to run. So let's say there are 200 or more wild horses running for their lives and they come to a canyon. Well, all 200 of them can't fit through the opening, so they all crowd in tighter in an attempt to be one of the first ones through. If their natural instinct were to move away from pressure, as soon as one of the horses pushed against another, that other horse would cease pushing and trying to get through the opening. He would also be the first one to be eaten by the predators. His instinct to survive makes moving away from pressure an unnatural thing for the horse. Because it is not natural for him, it is something he has to be taught.

I use a lariat to teach a horse about pressure. I place the lariat around his neck and use the slightest amount of pressure possible to get him to move in my direction. I am requesting a response in the form of movement. If I ask him to move and he doesn't, I'll hold the pressure until he does. He will start to get uncomfortable enough to move if I am patient enough to wait for that to happen. When the horse moves forward, the pressure is released immediately and completely. I'll give him a few minutes to think about it and then I'll ask him again. Each time I request, his response gets faster, which means the release comes sooner. In time, if I am consistent enough his response will become almost automatic.

I use a lariat to teach the horse about pressure and to get used to things up above him. Horse owned by Julia Brown.

I will also use the lariat to teach the colt he can be touched all over his body without harm. Horse owned by Julia Brown.

Rewarding my student for a job well done.

Helping my student grasp the concept of physical pressure.

I also use the lariat to teach the colt that he can be touched all over his body without harm. I'll rub him all over both sides of his body with the coiled rope. At no time do I hit him with the rope. If he becomes frightened, I'll stop, let him collect his thoughts, and then start again. Gradually I slip the lariat over his head and ask him to lead. I do not tie the colt while I am rubbing him with the rope. I want him to make the decision to stay around long enough to realize the rope isn't going to hurt him. If he wants to move or back up while I am rubbing him with the rope, I don't try to stop him. I just move with him and keep rubbing. I don't stop rubbing him until he stops moving his feet, then I'll stop rubbing him for a minute, and then rub him again.

If a horse becomes frightened when he is tied up he is more likely to panic because his means of escape has been blocked. He may hurt himself or me in his fight to escape. His panic shuts down all his learning channels. He has only one thing on his mind . . . escape.

I never force a horse to accept the rope; I ask him. Throughout the entire process I am constantly teaching the horse by asking him. I use the three R's when I teach the horse to respond to the rope, whether it is around his head like a halter or around his hindquarters like a harness. When I apply pressure, that's a request. When I get the correct response, I release. If I release the pressure for an incorrect response, the next time I ask, I'll get that same wrong response. The horse has either learned to do the wrong thing or he's confused. The next time you make the request, he will not know what to do.

When I begin riding the colt I teach the same thing. Picking up a bridle rein is a request. When he responds by moving his nose in the direction of the bridle rein, I'll release him. Remember, the horse will always go back to the point at which the release occurred, or to the action where he found relief from pressure. So, it is important not to release him until he gives the correct response. Remember, too, that horses are a lot like people—they are all looking for a point in their life where there is no pressure. Allow him to look and reward him when he finds it.

INTRODUCING THE PAD AND SADDLE

Once a horse is accustomed to the rope, it is time to introduce him to the saddle pad. It is important to go slowly enough that you do not frighten him, but not so slowly as to cause him to be suspicious. His suspicions may lead to a fearful reaction on his part. At this point the colt is not tied up, so he is free to take off running if that is what he wants to do. Place the rope around his neck so you can control the direction in which he moves, but

Once the horse is accustomed to the rope, it is time to introduce him to the saddle pad.

After the horse has accepted the pad, I introduce him to the saddle, using the same slow and steady manner.

don't try to stop him from moving. If he takes off, use the rope to pull him around in a circle so he can face his fear of the pad. If he dumps the pad in the dirt, just pick it up and start all over again. Don't make a big deal out of it. Rub him all over with the pad so he can see it will not hurt him no matter where it touches his body. Then place it on his back and ask him to walk a few steps with it in place. If he runs out from under it, again, it's no big deal. Just pick it up, dust it off, and start again. Don't go to the next step until he has accepted the pad.

Once the horse has accepted the pad, introduce him to the saddle in the same manner—slow and steady, always aware of his feelings and fears. If you take things slowly horses generally remain receptive to what you ask of them throughout their training. You will save time in the long run because you will not have to go back and repeat any of the lessons already taught.

I have one hard and fast rule about the colt's first saddling. Before I saddle a colt for the very first time, I always try to borrow someone else's saddle. When it is on his back, I first pull the cinch up without fastening it. I want to see what kind of reaction I get. Either I have to go pick the saddle up out of the dirt and start again—which is why it is important that you use someone else's saddle—or I can go on with the next part of the lesson. I cinch the saddle up slowly, but tightly enough that it will not fall off and allow the horse to buck the first time he is saddled (that is the only time he will be allowed to buck). Remember, the horse is naturally claustrophobic and the saddle is confining and restricting. Remember, too, his inherent fear of things above him. The saddle may seem like

The horse's natural instinct is to get rid of the saddle, so prepare yourself for his reaction to it to be a violent one.

the mountain lion that has pounced upon him from the rocks and is now having him for lunch. He has discovered he can't run from it so he feels he has to fight it. He does so by bucking. His natural instinct is to get rid of that saddle, so prepare yourself for his reaction to be a violent one.

I want the horse to learn that the saddle isn't going to hurt him and that it isn't going anywhere. Once he realizes this he will usually stop bucking. If I allow him to buck each time he is saddled, he will think it is a routine part of the program and bucking becomes a habit. I don't want that to happen. After he has stopped bucking and is calm and collected, I proceed with the lesson.

TEACHING THE HORSE TO ACCEPT THE ROPE AROUND HIS FOOT

The next lesson to teach the colt is to get used to a rope around his foot. This one lesson will teach him several very important things. First, it reinforces what he has learned about giving to pressure. When I pull on the rope and he makes a move in my direction, I release the pressure. I do not send him running off around the round pen and then yank his foot away from him. The only thing that would teach him is fear. If you plan to put your horse into any kind of a training program that involves the use of a rope, the last thing you need is for him to be afraid of the rope. I don't want my horses to be afraid. I want them to look for me when they are afraid and know I will help them.

Second, getting used to a rope around his foot helps the horse get accustomed to being hobbled should he ever need hobbling. This is a valuable lesson if you plan to do a lot of trail riding. It also helps him get used to having his feet picked up by the farrier. Contrary to popular belief it is not the farrier's job to teach a horse how to stand on three legs (for a young horse this can be a terrifying situation). By the same token, if my farrier ever wants to find out how fast he can be fired, just let him whack my horse with a rasp for not standing still while he is holding my horse's foot up in his hand. Finally, this lesson will teach the horse to stand quietly and not panic if he should ever become entangled in a piece of wire. This one lesson can and often does save a ton of money in vet bills. Occasionally it even saves the life of the horse. I never work on the lesson with the rope for more than ten or fifteen minutes because of the horse's anxiety level. It is well worth a few moments of discomfort in a controlled situation like this for me to have peace of mind that my horse will not tear his leg off if he ever gets it caught in something out in the pasture. Also, I can feel safer riding on the trail knowing he will not panic and do something to injure one or both of us if he gets his feet caught in a vine.

I turned two of my geldings out into a paddock behind my house this past summer after a long road trip. They were excited to be able to stretch their legs and started to run and play. The younger one chased the older one around the paddock; then the older one went off in pursuit of the younger one. The young gelding ran into a corner of the fence and before he could get turned around to run back out he discovered the older horse had been following too closely. In an effort to keep himself from being pushed through the fence, he reared up just enough to keep his front end out of the fence

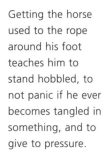

Getting the horse used to the rope around his foot teaches him to stand hobbled, to not panic if he ever becomes tangled in something, and to give to pressure.

when the other horse plowed into him. The older horse stopped, but as the young horse came down both front feet went between the strands of wire. To maintain his balance, he shuffled his back feet forward to get them under himself and managed to get one back foot over the bottom strand of wire.

Now this horse was in a world of trouble, as he was completely entangled in wire that could have ripped him to shreds if he had panicked and fought. Fortunately, I saw the whole incident and was already on my way with the wire cutters, but the young gelding never moved. He stood and allowed me to pick up his feet and place them on the proper side of the wire. His only injury was two small punctures from the barbs on the wire on one rear hoof. I am convinced the outcome would have been much more tragic and costly had I not taken the time to teach him to get used to having a rope around his foot.

As you can see, everything I do with horses prepares them for another lesson a little farther down the road.

MOUNTING AND RIDING

Before I climb in the saddle I want the horse standing quietly and squarely. I want to be able to crawl all over him without him moving. I want him to stand while I get on and off from both sides of the saddle. From day one I get my horses used to being mounted, dismounted, and fooled with on both sides. Whatever I do to him on the left side, I also do on the right. This is called balancing up your horse. It is important that you remember to do it because horses don't have spines, they have solid walls down the middle of their backs. Whatever you do on the left doesn't automatically get through to the other side of his brain. You will have to introduce him to everything twice, once from the left and then again from the right. It will, at times, be like working with two completely different horses because he will often react differently to having things done on one side or the other. But, if you will balance up your horse in the beginning, should you ever find yourself in a situation where you have to mount on the right side, your horse will not object.

While the horse is standing quietly, put your weight in the stirrup and gradually work your way up into the saddle. Sit down gently. Don't just haul yourself up and plop all your weight down in the middle of his back all at once. Give him a chance to get used to the weight and to something being above him before you ask anything else of him.

Then ask the horse to move out at a walk by applying pressure with your legs. If he doesn't move, squeeze harder or bump him a little with your legs. As soon as he moves, release the pressure. If he starts to buck, accept that it

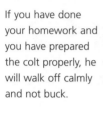

If you have done your homework and you have prepared the colt properly, he will walk off calmly and not buck.

is your own fault for not taking as much time as was necessary for him to grasp the concept. Back up and ask, "What part of the program did he not understand?"

If a horse gets scared his instinct will be to run. If you get scared because he is running and pull on the reins before he has been taught about stopping and control, then you block his means of escape. Shutting the door to his escape will cause him to go to plan B, which is to fight. He will fight by bucking. For this reason when I first get on a horse I've just started, I usually don't put anything on his face. If he gets scared while I am on him I would rather he run than buck. I can ride just as fast as he can run, but I don't ride the broncs so well anymore. I don't want anything on his face that will tempt me to pull on him while he is running. After a lap or two around the pen he will see that I won't hurt him and that he can't get rid of me and he'll stop. Once he stops, I'll rub him and let him calm down. Then, I will encourage him to move out at a walk again.

If you do your homework and prepare the colt properly, he will walk off calmly and not buck. Remember that you don't just walk out and climb aboard without properly explaining to him what it is you are about to do and taking his objections to your idea under consideration. It may take as long as two hours before you feel confident the horse trusts you and has understood your presentation. Just getting on the horse may be all you accomplish the first day. You must be willing to go at a pace the horse can accept and deal with. Once he is started under saddle he should be put into a consistent training program. Riding him is only part of the program. You shouldn't necessarily ride him every day, but he should be taught every day.

People think that if I take a horse to train for thirty days, he has to be ridden thirty days. That is not how my program works. He will probably have fifteen days of riding, but he will have thirty days of training. Being led quietly and calmly into the wash rack is part of his training. Standing tied quietly to the fence with his saddle on and waiting patiently for me to come and untie him is part of his training. Loading quickly, quietly, and willingly into the trailer is also part of his training. These are all things horses work on while they are in my program. Probably one day out of the week he will have a day off to be a horse. Kids get two days away from school every week. Most people get two days off from work every week, and as much as I love working with horses, even I like a day off occasionally. Why should you expect your horse to be any different? Working a horse seven days a week for thirty, sixty, or ninety days or more will cause him to become soured, ill-tempered, and difficult to handle. His bucket gets too full and you have to give him an opportunity to get some of the water out before you try to put more in.

STOPPING ON WHOA

The most important prerequisite for any horse-training program—the very first thing you absolutely must have before you can teach your horse anything—is forward motion from the horse. You can't teach a horse anything if he won't move his feet. You can't even teach him to stop if he won't go someplace. Once he starts to move his feet, then you can begin to work on controlling where he puts them. Keep in mind that you want to be the pilot, not the passenger. Always remember that the horse that will buck you off is the horse that won't go anywhere. Forward motion is an essential part of any training program.

After the horse has developed forward motion, most people make the mistake of using the word "whoa" much too soon in their teaching program, before the horse has learned to understand its meaning. They get the horse going forward and then start telling him to whoa. The horse, not knowing what the word means, keeps going and they keep hollering whoa. He eventually thinks that whoa means go. If, to make matters worse, someone runs around behind flailing his arms and hollering whoa, the horse thinks whoa means go faster, and go faster he does, whenever he hears whoa.

The way I teach "whoa," or how to stop on the whoa command, is to put the horse in the round pen and get him moving around it. I'll step toward his shoulder and ask him to stop one time. If he doesn't stop I just move him around the pen some more and try again. Pretty soon moving around the pen ceases to be fun and starts to be work and the horse will want to stop. I allow him to do so by moving to his shoulder again and asking him to stop. As soon as all of his feet quit moving I say, "Whoa." Then, I will move him around the pen again and repeat the process. Soon he begins to associate the word whoa with break time, stop, take a breath, and it becomes a good thing. It means something that will make him comfortable. When you are trying to teach your horse what whoa means, if you say it and he doesn't stop, don't keep on saying it. Whoa is one word, period. It's not whoa, please. It's not whoa, damn it, and it's not whoa, whoa, whoa.

Once you have taught your horse how to stop and you have a little control over his speed and direction, you will be able to head off a lot of potential wrecks long before they have the opportunity to materialize. I always want my horse to stay soft, so I don't pull on his face. I just take the slack out of the reins. If you spend enough time teaching your horse what you want from him and allow him enough time to give you what you are asking, taking the slack out of the reins is all you should ever need to stop him.

You can't make a horse stop if he doesn't want to. There isn't a bit severe enough to stop a horse that doesn't want to stop. You might use a bit with enough leverage to break his jaw but it will only make him run faster. You can't make him stop, but you can do two things: You can control his direction and you can make him want to stop.

Sam gets the colt used to the rope all around him.

You get the horse to stop by working with his mind and controlling where he puts his feet. If your horse wants to trot when you want him to walk, or he wants to lope when you want him to trot, just pull him off to the side in a small circle until he slows down. When he does slow down, ride him off again. If he starts to speed up, repeat the process until he slows down again. It's hard work and uncomfortable for him to travel in that little circle. Be consistent in asking him to slow down and soon just picking up the bridle rein will be enough cue to slow him down. He will think, "No, I don't want to go around in any more of those awful circles," and he will slow down before you really have to ask him. Remember, you are the pilot, not the passenger, and you need to be the one to decide speed and direction—not the horse. You can't make him stop moving his feet, but at least you can learn how to control the direction and speed at which he moves them.

THE HORSE'S RESPONSE

Watching other people ride will help you understand how a horse responds to different requests. Watch a horse that has been asked to do a lead change and take note of what position he is in when he makes a pretty one and what position he's in when he fumbles. Look where his feet are when the rider asks him to do something. Studying what is known as "form to function" will help you understand why a horse has to be in a certain position in order to correctly execute certain maneuvers. Don't just ask your horse to do something without considering whether he has had adequate time to set himself up to do what you have asked. For example, before you mount, be sure he is square; otherwise he will have to move his feet to maintain his balance while you get on.

Listen to your horse. Understand his uncertainties and try to show him what you expect from him in a way he can comprehend. By doing this you will have a horse that will try his best to please you and become your loyal companion.

The whole world is trying to solve its problems with a get-a-gun mentality. Everyone is trying to force everyone else to see things from their own point of view. Cases of domestic violence, child abuse, and terrorism are at an all-time high. People think that the problems they are having with their horses can be solved by pulling harder on their faces, wearing spurs with sharper rowels and using them more often, or going to a crueler means or methods.

I can walk into a pen with a wild horse and within two hours communicate my ideas to him in a way he understands. Within two hours I can have him respect me enough to listen and trust me enough to allow me to put a saddle and rider on him for the first time. Predator can teach prey, with little or no protest on the part of the prey, to go against his inborn instinct for survival and to trust that no harm will come to him. The horse has been allowed to make mistakes without punishment and he has been rewarded for every effort he made to get it right. He has been allowed to be fearful of new situations while receiving assurance that I will help him work through his fear. All I have to do is keep showing him that I am his friend and that I will do nothing to cause him to hurt himself.

Knowing this, why can't we humans get past racial issues and cultural and socioeconomic differences and find a way to understand each other and reach compromises without wars and uprisings? If one person can find a better way of communicating with his partner, whether that partner be animal or human—a way that is based on respect, trust, and understanding—then perhaps that age-old dream of peace on earth can become a reality before it is too late.

Horseman or Trainer
Which One for You?

Forty years ago I wanted to compete on the roping, reining, and cutting horse circuits and I wanted my horse to make me look like a great trainer. I tried every gimmick I could find, new bits, tie downs, side pulls, anything that promised a quick fix to the current problem at hand.

I have met some great horsemen in my travels across the country and around the world. These men did not consider themselves trainers and they did not care about competition. They cared about their horses and just wanted them to be as good as possible. These horsemen, along with the teachings of my father, eventually enabled me to see the horse in a completely different light. Instead of comparing one horse to another in competition, I began to look at them as individuals. I set out to do as the Army slogan suggests: help them be all they could be.

For many years I worked with only the horse and not the rider. I was just a trainer. Later, I came to realize how pointless it was for me to work with a horse and send him home to an owner who could not or would not communicate with him. The horse with which I had worked to establish a relationship based on respect and trust went home to find his life uncomfortable and unpleasant. As a result I decided to try teaching people how to work with their own horses. Now I teach people to understand the true nature of the horse, how to communicate with him in his language, and, finally, how to gain his respect and trust.

A relationship with a horse that is based on respect and trust is easier for everyone concerned than one that is based on a chain of command. Most people soon realize that these same simple ideas and techniques can be used to improve their human relationships as well. Every time I work with a horse and help him get better or work through a specific problem, I see a connection to a human problem. Sometimes the owners realize that they, not the horse, are the reason for the problem the horse is having. For instance, people who keep a tight rein on their horses and constantly correct them for the slightest infraction tend to be very controlling in their personal relationships as well. This type of observation has given me some insight as to why I've had problems in some of my relationships in the past, whether the relationships were business or personal, animal or human.

HORSEMEN HELP HORSES UNDERSTAND PEOPLE

What I do with the horses can be summed up by a phrase from the movie *The Horse Whisperer*. I don't help people with horse problems; I help horses with people problems. To take the explanation a bit farther, I try to help the people understand how they are causing their horses to have problems and how to become part of the solution rather than part of the problem.

At my clinics I don't tell people how to make a horse lope a circle, stop, back up, or turn around over his hocks. What I do is explain the horse's mind and how it functions. I want the people to have an understanding of what is going on in the horse's mind so they can go home and think about what they need to do to get the horse to understand what it is they want from him.

I usually have a limited time frame in which to work the horses at my clinics. Because I do not hand pick them or resume them in, the only promise I can make to the owner regarding his progress is that the horse will be as good as he is capable of becoming in the time I have to work with him. I am not a magician and I can only take the horse as far as he is physically and mentally capable of going. I am amused by people who seem to think that if the horse meets or surpasses their expectations it is because he is an exceptional horse, but if I tell them he will never make a world champion cutter, reiner, or barrel horse, it must be because I am not a capable horse person. It almost seems as though these people would rather pay me to ruin their horse by trying to make him something he will never be as long as I tell them what they want to hear.

Generally, by the end of a two-hour clinic the horse has been successfully started, saddled and ridden. Occasionally I'll have one that isn't even halter broke and I'll add fifteen to thirty extra minutes to the program. What people need to realize is that having a horse successfully started in two hours entails a lot more than most folks are able to comprehend. Also, having a horse started and ridden one time is a far cry from having one broke to ride. Once I have started the colt it is the owner's responsibility to go on with him and see to it that he completes his education. If I start a colt at one of my clinics and the owner takes him home, kicks him out into the pasture and never even looks at him for another six months, it is not fair to me or to the horse to blame either of us if that owner gets his butt dumped in the dirt the next time he tries to ride the horse.

Virtually anyone can take a horse and have him saddled and ridden in thirty minutes or less. It all depends upon how much of a rodeo you want. Chances are better than average that the horse hasn't learned anything at the end of the session, and most people watching the ordeal haven't learned anything either. Chances are also that the experience has not been a pleasant one for the horse or the rider. The horse will remember how unpleasant that first saddling was and consequently any future saddling will be just as unpleasant for both of you because of it.

I have noticed that we spend a lot of time teaching people how to ride but we never teach them how to be horsemen, and the horse suffers for it. We tell riders to use a bit in the horse's mouth without teaching them why they should use it, how to use it correctly, or what happens if it is used incorrectly. Before you can teach your horse to be a winner it is important that you first learn to become a horseman. Learning to ride is only a tiny aspect. You should learn to understand the horse and how to get the most from him in a willing manner. There is much more involved in responsible horse ownership than could ever be contained in one book or taught by one person. You owe it to your horse to become the best that you can be if you expect him to be the best that he can be.

A GOOD HORSEMAN MAKES TIME TO LEARN

I cannot ever remember a time when I did not want to be a cowboy. As a boy I spent time learning whatever I could by working on farms and ranches after school, on weekends and during the summer. As a young man with a family to support I worked two, sometimes three, jobs at a time. But I still found time during the twenty-four hour course of a day to study my passion. I found an hour at two A.M. to experiment with a new technique or twenty minutes after my lunch break to study the veterinary journals. A man approached me after one of my clinics this past year and made the comment that he would do anything to be able to do what I do with the horses. I told him I did not think he would. He seemed puzzled, but if you think about it, I was being honest with him.

If you have a passion for doing something and you want to do it badly enough, you will find away to get it done. There is a difference between wanting something passionately and just wishing for it. Whenever people talk to me about learning more about their horses, one of the most common responses I hear is, "I just don't have the time." What they are really telling me is that they are not willing to do whatever it takes to make the time. My dad told me a long time ago that if you want to do something badly enough, if you are really dedicated to learning something, you will find the time.

When I was a young man wanting very much to be a cowboy, I had an opportunity to do some day work on a big cattle outfit out west during their round-up and shipping time. Back then most all the large ranches hired day workers and the pay was ten dollars a day. I was told to be at the barn, saddled up and ready to go at four A.M. the next day. Since I had about an hour's drive to the ranch I had to get up at one A.M. to get my horse fed, get my old one-horse trailer hooked up behind my '52 Dodge pickup, and drive out to the ranch. I got up, got my chores done, hooked up and took off. I was so excited about being one of the hands on this outfit that I was wide-eyed and bushy-tailed even at two in the morning. I made it to the barn in plenty of time, unloaded, saddled up, and was waiting to start at four A.M. so we could be at the back side of the pasture before first light and before the cattle went into the brush.

We started gathering cattle and around eleven A.M. we had a pretty good-sized bunch of cows headed for the working pens. This particular pasture was about nine thousand acres so it took a little while to drive the herd of cattle to the pens. We had a number of what are known as herd quitters trying to get back to the brush. By about one P.M. we had them in the pens and counted, but we were still forty or fifty short. The boss told us we needed to go back and find them while the ranch hands started sorting and working the ones we had gathered.

At three or four in the afternoon one of the other day workers and I drove in a little handful of cattle that we had found bunched up in the brush. Remember, I was young, eager and really wanting to be a cowboy. In my excitement about my first day I had forgotten a few important necessities like a canteen of water and a few snacks in my saddlebags. I had been horseback for twelve hours. I was thirsty and my stomach was growling loud enough to spook every cow in the pens. I rode over to the boss and inquired as to how much longer he thought it would be before we were finished. He looked at me and asked if I was one of the day workers. I replied, "Yes, sir." He calmly responded, "Well, son, there's twenty-four hours in a day so you're just about half done."

I think back on this occasionally and realize that it taught me a lot about the concept of time, especially when it came to finding enough of it to do the things I really wanted to do. This experience went a long way towards teaching me that there are twenty-four hours in a day, not eight like a lot of people seem to think.

I have spent a great deal of time and money on my education as a horseman. No, I did not receive formal training from a big university, but I have invested over forty years in the school of hard knocks and practical application, seven days a week. I have spent countless hours observing and studying horses and everything about them. I have spent a small fortune on doctor bills and vet bills, learning how not to do some things. In the end, the education I have received and continue to receive every day from horses is what I need to be able to teach other people how to improve the quality of life for their horses.

The number of horses that are abused through acts of deliberate cruelty represents a small percentage in comparison to those that are abused as a result of ignorance on the part of those who are supposed to care for them. My goal is to educate people enough to help make them think about every aspect of horse ownership. I want you to walk a mile in your horse's shoes and try to learn to think like a horse so you can figure out what is really best for your horse instead what makes you feel better.

Although I have been studying horses for over forty years now, I am the first to admit that I still have a lot to learn. Every horse I work with teaches

To a horse that is well trained it makes no difference if you are riding English or Western. Here Sam puts Rooster through some of his dressage maneuvers while riding Western. It's all about putting the buttons in the right places and using them correctly.

me something new. I spent a great deal of time in the beginning doing things wrong, but that has only made me more determined to learn how to do things the right way. Doing things right has meant arming myself with as much knowledge as I possibly can about horses and being willing to admit that I did not always know what I know now.

In 1985, the Mullendore Ranch had just received a shipment of expensive new horses that had to be started and I was determined to put some of my new knowledge to work and ride one without breaking it. I got permission from the horse division manager to try a different approach. I put a colt in the round pen and walked in with it, feeling my way through a curious mental waltz with an animal that wanted no part of me. All during that first day the horse ran whenever I approached.

I tried to get him to stop and face me, to 'hook up' with me mentally. The other cowboys observing the process teased me mercilessly. I might as well have been wearing a dress out there! By the second day the colt was convinced that I was not a particular threat to him. He also realized that running in circles was not exactly what he wanted or needed to do.

When the colt stopped and looked at me I turned and walked away from him. Turning my back to him told the colt that I was the dominant player on

This colt is contemplating leaving town but decides to stay where things have been pretty quiet thus far—with me.

the field. If he turned his rear end to me in any shape, form or fashion I threw dirt clods at his feet, clapped my hands or did whatever it took to make him feel uncomfortable. Facing me had to be the colt's idea, and he would have to figure out that turning his butt to me was not a good idea. If he wanted to run, that was fine. I let him run. I would keep him running until he figured out it was a lot easier to just stand and look at me, but the decision was always his. After that I could approach and touch him, and when I walked away from him the colt would follow. Some kind of strange mental connection had been made.

By the third day I could stand near the colt and touch him all over. I had even saddled him without having inflicted pain of any kind and without having run the risk of injury to the colt or to myself as I had in the past. But there was still more to do. I put a saddle pad and saddle on the colt and, after he calmed down, I stroked his neck and spoke soothingly to him. The other cowboys knew what I was about to do and made a point of telling me what a fool I was. I knew they might be right, but I also knew that so far this had been a lot easier than the way we had been doing it. The colt stood stock-still. Since he was not wearing a halter, bridle, or anything on his head, I could only hope he would respond to my touch. I put my foot in the stirrup, slowly stepped up, and sat down in the saddle. I reached out and tapped him on the neck and he walked to the other side of the pen and stopped. When I touched him again he walked back to the other side of the pen.

This was the first horse I had ever used this method with, and he went

My student gets used to being touched all over with the rope. I do not use the rope to create fear or inflict pain.

on to win over $100,000.00 in competition on the cutting horse circuit. I did not break that horse; I formed a partnership with him. That day this rugged, untamed cowboy, who had previously placed no value on tenderness, patience, or kindness, climbed into a round pen with a wild horse, befriended it, and climbed out a different man. I was no longer just a trainer. I was no longer just a cowboy. I was a kinder man, a gentler man; I was on my way towards becoming a horseman.

With each subsequent horse, I refined the technique and learned what worked and what did not. I was able to compress the amount of time it took for the horse to hook up with me mentally in order to earn his respect and trust. The technique took on almost transcendental qualities. I learned how to stop a horse's forward motion by stepping into his line of view. I discovered that approaching the animals with an open hand frightened them, while holding up one finger as a small focal point did not. Charging at a horse that threatened to charge me was difficult at first, but it was also a part of this kind of ceremonial laying on of hands, with the sole objective of gaining the animal's respect and trust.

It took six or seven years for me to be completely comfortable with what I was doing; to get over the macho cowboy stuff and realize that I could teach the horses much better without it. Using this technique has given me an inner strength, a confidence in myself without being arrogant or belligerent. It has helped me as much as any horse I have worked with. When I walk into that round pen with a horse, regardless of the reason he is there, I have to believe I am the best horseman there is without being egotistical about it because the horse has to believe it, too. If I don't believe it, the horse won't either, and if I am a snob about it all the talent and ability in the world will not help me get close to a horse that doesn't want to have anything to do with me and my egotistical attitude. My technique teaches the horse to respond without physically making him do anything.

There are a great many books on the market about training horses and riding them. The problem is that they cover one subject or the other, but few of them cover both in conjunction with one another. In order to become a good horseman you need to work on teaching yourself and your horse at the same time. It is not possible to properly train a horse if you don't know how to ride, nor can you safely ride a horse that has not been properly trained. Time and time again I see trainers who work with the horse but offer no suggestion to the person who is going to be riding the horse after he is trained. I see riding instructors teaching their students to post on the diagonal, square their shoulders and such, but I don't see any of them teaching their students about working with their horse.

Many of the training books you buy tell what to do but they don't tell you how to do it, or what to do if things don't go according to plan. You may start the book at the beginning, but because you get bored or you can't understand it, you skip a few chapters. Then, when you start trying to teach your horse something from the book, the horse gets confused because he didn't get to read the book and you missed some vital information in the chapters that you skipped. All of your great ideas for your horse mean nothing if your horse doesn't understand them.

This past year I received a phone call from a man who had purchased my Teaching by Asking video at one of my clinics. He told me that he had been bucked off and broken both of his arms while trying to use my technique, and he wanted to know if I thought he had done something wrong. I was certain he had, but I did not know if I would be able to figure out what it was over the phone. Further inquiry into his method revealed that he had fast-forwarded the tape to what he referred to as "the good part." I told him that was his first and biggest mistake and any subsequent mistakes which led to his mishap could be attributed to that one.

PAIR THE HORSE WITH THE RIDER

A very large majority of my current clients are first-time horse owners. I commend those of them who are willing to admit they know absolutely nothing about horses and make an honest effort to learn things that will help them properly care for their horses. If you are thinking about purchasing a horse for the first time, or you are going back into the horse world after a long sabbatical, consider the fact that your first horse should be your teacher, not your student. An older, well-trained, well-mannered horse is what I recommend for a first timer. A person who knows nothing about horses has no business with a young green-broke horse that doesn't know anything about anything. If you purchase such a horse, lacking the knowledge you need to teach that horse, how do you think he will learn anything? If you don't know how to teach him, how will you know if he has learned, and how will you know whether what he learned was right or wrong? The ultimate result of such a union is frustration on both parts because neither has the skills necessary to bridge the communication gap. It can also result in serious injury to the horse, the rider, or both because the rider's increasing anxiety level will cause an increase in the anxiety level of the horse (as was described in Chapter One). Sequentially, the rider ends up getting rid of his horse by any means he can and getting out of the horse business altogether.

An older horse can teach a novice rider how to ask for what he wants without getting all bent out of shape if the request isn't perfect. He can teach the novice how to handle small upsets without getting him hurt. This, in turn, builds the confidence of the novice rider to the point that he is then able to handle more serious situations without losing his cool or getting hurt. An older horse can teach you how to stay out of trouble and how to stop a wreck before it happens. It is not enough for you to know how to climb aboard and hang on. You might do that time and time again, but sooner or later you'll find yourself in a situation where you don't know what to do. The outcome of such a situation will be a lot less tragic if you are on a horse that does.

As you become a better, more experienced and more confident rider, you can consider working with younger and more inexperienced horses. You will have something to offer them that will help make them better, calmer horses. You will know how and what to teach the young horse. Always remember that the teaching process should be slow, steady and continuous. Your presentation to the horse determines whether or not he will understand. If he is frightened, he will never understand. You must learn to present things to him in a way he can tolerate until he can understand.

It is not a good idea to work with your horse if you are in a bad mood or if you are in a hurry. Your horse will pick up on this and be easily frightened. You would be much better off spending that extra fifteen minutes before you have to leave for the airport making sure you have everything you need for your trip rather than trying to teach your horse. Always be cognizant of your mental state before you work with your horse. If you've just had a big fight with your boss or mate, do your horse a favor and take a long walk before you visit with him.

One of the most important things you can do for your horse before you start schooling him is to have some idea of what you want him to do. Ninety-nine percent of horses are trainable to some degree. The problem is that most owners' expectations far exceed the horse's capabilities. A good horseman designs a program to fit whatever horse he happens to be working with at the time. He takes into account the horse's mental and physical capabilities and overall structure before he designs a program. Most trainers, on the other hand, take a horse and try to mold him to fit a predesigned program without considering whether he is mentally, physically or structurally capable of achieving the goals the trainer has set for him. That is why it is so important to know what you want from a horse even before you make the purchase.

If you are looking for a reining horse prospect, don't go out and purchase a horse that is straight-shouldered, high-hocked, and wide-chested. If you ask a horse built like this to spin or slide to a stop it will be difficult because he is not structurally designed to do it. He can be taught to do it just as a football linebacker can be taught to dance the ballet, but it will always be difficult for him and it will never be pretty. By the same token, you should not take the ballerina reining horse out for an endurance ride. This is where you need the stocky, big-boned, wide-chested horse you might have previously been considering for reining.

I never want to bruise a colt's ego or cause him to become confused or unsure of himself. I don't want to destroy his confidence by asking him to do something he is not physically or mentally capable of doing. That's why it is important to progress slowly. If you begin working with a barrel horse and you teach him to run really, really fast around the barrels but you have not taken the time to put a solid foundation on him, if he consistently runs a fifteen-second pattern but also quite consistently knock the barrels over, what have you accomplished? Remember: Slow and correct will beat fast and wrong every time.

THREE THINGS THAT MAKE YOU A BETTER HORSEMAN

As you work toward becoming a better horseman, consider doing three things that will help you tremendously. First, you must have more patience than you ever thought possible. Without it you will not find a place in the horse world. You must be patient enough to take whatever time is needed to teach your horse what it is you want him to learn. You will have to be patient enough to learn what you need to know in order to teach him properly. And patience will be required from you in order to help your horse work through his fears.

Second, you will have to become extremely open minded. Horse people in general tend to be very closed-minded and quite prejudiced. Quarter Horse people seem to only notice Quarter Horses, Walking Horse people are inclined to appreciate only Walking Horses, and so on. There are people who claim to appreciate all of the breeds but they only like black horses or bays or sorrels. I am not a Quarter Horse person; I am a horse person, period. A good horseman appreciates all breeds and colors as horses first, and whatever else they might be is secondary.

The part of the horse that a true horseman works with is virtually the same in all horses regardless of breed or color. That part is his brain. If you were to dissect a Walking Horse and an Arabian and place their brains side by side on an exam table, you would not be able to distinguish which was which. It is man who has created the different packaging the horses come in now, but what is inside the different packages is still pretty much the same.

The third thing you must develop is a willingness to get rid of your ego. You will have to realize that all horses can't do all maneuvers well. Focus on the positive aspects of each horse as an individual and reward him for the smallest effort he makes to do something right. You will have to consider your inability to teach rather than your horse's inability to learn if things don't go according to plan. If your horse bucks you off, you need to ask yourself, "What part of the program did I not explain thoroughly enough to him?"

If you have a horse that genuinely tries to do everything you ask him to do but all you see is that he does not do it fast enough or pretty enough, then you have a horse that will never please you. People who can only focus on the bad things their horses do are usually the people who have bad horses, because that is what they expect to have. If your horse makes a mistake, you have to be willing to look at yourself as the probable cause of it. Maybe you taught him incorrectly or you don't know how to ask him properly for what you want. It could be simply that you did not take enough time to prepare him for this step and he is unsure, or a whole host of other things you may not have thought about.

Horses aren't dumb. In many ways they are much smarter than humans. Time after time I have watched them walk right to a gate built into a round pen that looked exactly like the rest of the panels and that I could not find myself. I try to teach people about thinking like a horse. If you will try to do than, then you won't think he is dumb, because you will not be asking him to do something that is unnatural for him.

Over the past ten years of working with horses and people I have learned that there are two aspects to every situation I encounter with a horse—facts and opinions. The only things the people have regarding the situations are their opinions. If I want the facts, I have to talk to the horse. He will tell me what I need to know and he will always be straightforward and to the point. He does not tell me verbally, nor does he tell me with some form of mental telepathy. He tells me what I need to know by the way he stands, by the look in his eye, by the way he carries himself, and by the way he moves and acts. The horses speak volumes to me and I listen and watch very carefully. This is not necessarily easy because horses are non verbal, but it can be compared to the way a mother knows by her child's actions when something is not right. She often knows by the way her baby cries whether he is wet, tired, hungry, or sick. All of these cries sound different. It takes careful observation and close attunement with horses to develop this kind of understanding. Anyone who is willing to put forth the time and effort can learn to do exactly the same thing.

Everything I have learned about horses I can pretty well apply to people. You don't control a horse with a bit; you control him with his mind. As my father tried to tell me, rough and tough isn't the way to get it done. If I had listened to him years ago I am sure I would have been different in all my relationships, whether human or animal, business or personal.

HORSEMEN DO NOT RELY ON GIMMICKS

Horses experience many of the same emotions as humans. They get angry and confused and they respond similarly to stimuli. The key is to figure out how to stimulate them to the proper response. I don't recommend the use of gimmicks for this purpose. I don't use draw reins or running martingales because they take away the rider's need to think about what she is doing. The rider needs to be able to get the horse to flex at the poll and give lateral movement without a gimmick to do it for her. I want my horse to learn what I am trying to teach him. I also want my clients to learn what I am trying to teach them, so I don't use gimmicks on them either. I use a straightforward, simple approach with my clients just as I do with the horses.

Some of the gadgets that I refer to as gimmicks are tack collars, high port, long shank bits, mechanical contrivances with cables and pulleys, and any other torture device that was designed to make your horse perform like a world champion whether he is one or not.

Years ago we used the running W. It worked great in the hands of those who knew what they were doing, but it was a total disaster for those who did not. Things like the quick-stop devices that have a nutcracker effect on the horse's lower jaw can be a handy item if the rider is aware of the fact that he can't pull on the reins with the same amount of force he previously used with a snaffle bit. If he does, the rider will probably have his horse in his lap after he pulls the horse over on top of him. If the horse you are using the quick stop on isn't trained to neck rein there isn't any lateral control to help out in the way of steering. Using a tack collar to make your horse neck rein or back up can put your horse in your lap in much the same way if you are very heavy handed. I have seen some horsemen use a spade bit and have the horse responding beautifully, like a well-oiled machine. I had to look really closely to see the rider's hands move. That same bit in the hands of heavy handed Jerky Joe will inflict more pain and torment on the horse than the dungeons and torture chambers of the Middle Ages ever could.

Tie downs can be helpful if you are in an arena roping, but an absolute disaster if you are going trail riding. I have seen horses wearing tie downs on the trail bend their heads down to drink from a stream, stick a front foot through the tie down strap and have a real panic attack. If a horse loping along the trail gets a tree limb run through the tie down strap he can give you a change in direction much faster than you want.

The things I consider gimmicks are too numerous to name here. Before you go out and purchase tack, training devices, or gimmicks, I urge you to think about it, study it, and decide whether or not you really need it. Consider whether or not you know how to use it and what painful effect it might have on your horse if it is used incorrectly. I believe it will be much more beneficial to you and your horse if you spend more time teaching him what you want him to do. Learn how to ask him, then teach him how to do what you want in a way he can understand, rather than relying on the use of a device that will jar his pain sensors.

I have observed novice riders wearing what are known as 'rock grinder' spurs. The rowels on these spurs look like miniature Skil saw blades and are every bit as sharp. The riders go along absent-mindedly poking their horses with every step. They jab their horses to get them to move a hip over or to get a quicker lead departure. Blood dribbles down the horse's side and the riders proceed to tell me they have to use the spurs because their horses are numb-sided. I would be willing to bet money that if these riders observed old Numb Side in the pasture, they would see him try to get rid of every little green-headed fly that crawled up his rib cage. Perhaps the problem is not that the horses are numb-sided. It may be that these horses have not been taught how to move away from pressure. The riders should take their horses home and teach them, "Horse, when I put my leg against you, you move over."

Bits, spurs, and gimmicks are no better or worse than the person using them. The lightest, softest bit on the market can become a torture device in the hands of someone who doesn't know how to use it. Most fly-by-night trainers have extensive knowledge of how the use of gimmicks can make them look like great trainers, whether the gimmick is used properly or not. They are after that quick fix and instant gratification.

If you put draw reins on a horse, he will automatically break at the poll, but, when you take them off and pull on the bridle reins, his head goes in the air and you haven't accomplished anything. Gimmicks keep the horse from having to think and figure things out. The gimmick becomes a crutch and the horse learns to rely on the crutch. When the crutch is removed, the horse doesn't know what to do.

Sam and Rooster became fast friends and spent a great deal of time together on the road but Rooster is always ready to go to work when duty calls.

Instead, try applying a little pressure with the reins. As soon as the horse responds in the proper direction, release the pressure. Gradually ask him to flex at the poll without expecting him to do it all at once. If you expect him to do it all at once and you never take the pressure off, he has no way of knowing he has done what you want. At first, his progress must be measured in the most minuscule degrees and he must be rewarded for even a thought in the right direction. Otherwise he has no incentive to try again. Think of how you might react if you were continuously made to feel that nothing you did was right. At first you would probably try harder, but eventually you would stop trying and then you'd stop listening altogether to the person who was trying to get you to respond.

HORSEMEN DO NOT MAKE A HORSE DO ANYTHING

Recently, I stopped at a local feed and tack store to purchase some equine fly spray. I wandered around the store looking at all the tack. Some of what I saw was a true work of art. Some of it was an object of sheer torture. Most of it was a method of confusion for both the horse and the rider. As I stood there contemplating a particular piece of equipment and trying to decide which part of the horse's anatomy it was designed to be used on, another customer approached me and wanted to know if she could ask my advice. "Sure," I told her. People's questions never bother me (but sometimes my answers bother them).

She explained to me that her horse was having a problem, which, by the way, is how the majority of the questions I am asked begin. It is seldom, if ever, the person who is having the problem. I guess it is easier on a fragile ego to blame the problem on something or someone else. Anyway, as she explained it, her horse was having a problem stopping and she asked me to show her which bit she needed to buy to make her horse stop.

I was reminded of a time some forty years ago when I was working a few outside horses. I had encountered the same problem and was seeking the exact same solution as the lady in the store. I knew a man who lived in the area who was considered to be one of the best horsemen in the country and I decided to ask his advice. I called him on the phone and after a routine exchange of pleasantries I proceeded to tell him about the problem I was having with this horse. I asked him if he could please tell me what kind of bit I needed to make this rascal stop. There was silence on the other end of the line. Just as I was getting ready to repeat the question, the man replied, "Sure, son. You just need a bit more knowledge." Then he just hung up the phone.

Having been so rudely put down by this great horseman, my bruised ego and I sulked around the house for a day or two. Once I got past the anger and hurt feelings, I was able to think about what he had said and realized he was right. To begin with, my horse did not have a problem stopping. I had seen him run wide open out across the pasture, stick his butt in the ground, slide thirty feet to a stop, roll back over his hocks and lope off in the opposite direction. As I thought about it, it became pretty obvious the horse did not have a problem, I did. He already knew how to stop. What I needed was a line of communication between his brain and mine so that I could get him to stop when I asked him.

I relayed the story to the customer in the store and she went away determined to find that line of communication with her horse and get it opened up. Most of the problems people have with their horses, their mates, and all the others with whom they share their lives is the word "make." How can I make my horse stop? How can I make my horse lope? How can I make my horse turn around? If you will watch your horse playing out in the pasture with his mates most likely you will see him already doing all the things you are contemplating making him do.

When people consider trying to "make" a horse do something it usually involves the use of a gimmick and it is usually an ego-driven desire. We live in an ego-driven society. People feel the need to conquer their horses, to make them behave the way they want. They are so busy competing with others they never take the time to really notice their horses. They only see what they want.

In my younger days I worked on a very large ranch that raised a lot of really good horses and part of my job was starting the two-year-olds. I started the colts, rode them around a few times and they were sent to someone else for the finishing touches that would determine if they were futurity prospects and worthy of going on to the trainer. Like most young cowboys I wanted to finish some of the colts I had started. Back then starting colts wasn't considered to be anything special, all the recognition went to the people who trained and finished them.

Finally, when things were a little slow, I was given a couple of colts and my chance to make an impression. Neither colt was anything special but at long last I had something to hone my skills on. One of the colts had made really nice progress. I could lope him around the arena and when he stopped, he would stick his butt in the ground and make the prettiest little sliding stop you ever saw. I thought this was my chance to move up the ladder and get to finish more colts. I told the ranch manager that he needed to come and watch this colt that I had done such a good job on. He said that the ranch owner would be back the next day and the two of them would be out to look him over.

The next morning I had the colt saddled and warmed up and was riding him around the arena when my boss, the owner, and a man I recognized as one of the top trainers in the country drove up. Here was my big chance! As the three of them leaned on the fence, I loped the colt down the middle of the arena. I said, "Whoa," pulled on the bridle reins, and that colt jabbed his front feet in the ground, dumped me up on his neck and darned near jumped clear out from under me.

I gathered my wits and my reins and started loping him around again. I said, "Whoa," and the same thing happened. In fact it happened three or four more times before I looked over and saw my boss and the owner walking back to the truck shaking their heads. I was mad, embarrassed, humiliated, and I wanted to kill that dumb horse for making me look so stupid.

As I led the colt out of the arena I saw the trainer that I had so admired and wanted to impress still leaning on the fence watching. I felt lower than road kill. As I walked by him, he said, "Nice colt." I could only think, "Yeah, right." I told him I did not know what had happened because the colt had been stopping as close to perfect as you could get for the past two weeks, but with everyone watching he had just come untrained. He looked at me and very quietly told me what was wrong.

All the time I had been working this colt it had been just him and me. I worked him slow and easy, loped him around, sat down in my saddle, picked up the reins and asked him to stop. He did what came very natural to him without any interference from me. But, when the boss showed up and I thought I had my big chance to show off, I loped him around and tried to make him stop. Instead of setting it up for him and giving him a chance to get ready to do what was natural (get his butt in the ground and slide to a stop), my ego got in the way and I tried to *make* him stop.

Once this horseman spent a little time explaining this to me, I got back on the colt and we loped around again. This time I asked him to stop just as I had been doing for the past couple of weeks. He sat down and slid to a stop as pretty as a picture. The horseman looked at me and grinned and then told me something that went on to reshape my way of working with horses. He said, "Don't forget: Your horse is your partner. Work with him and he will work for you. Don't try to make him do things just to inflate your ego." Now, when I hear that word "make," I remember a young cowboy so anxious to make a good impression that he almost forgot his partner.

Last year I attended a roping event in the Nashville, Tennessee, area. I was astonished to see several obviously lame horses being forced to compete in the event. I have no way of knowing whether the riders were ignorant of the fact that their horses were lame, or whether they just cared more about the competition than about their horses. As these were all fairly seasoned riders, I suspect the latter. I would like to offer a word of wisdom about competition for those of you who are into competition of judged events. Remember: The winner of a judged event is based solely on one person's opinion of that horse at that particular time.

HORSEMEN DO IT SLOWLY AND CORRECTLY

We live in a world of instant gratification. People want what they want right now, not someday, not pretty soon, but immediately if not sooner. From buying a house to problem solving, people go after the quick fix. School kids don't seem to spend as much time solving complex math problems; they just whip out the handy dandy calculator and voilá, instant answer. I received a painful example of this fact recently during one of my many visits to a fast food restaurant while on a long road trip. The computerized cash registers were not working and my order totaled three dollars and eighty-six cents. I handed the lad a five-dollar bill and he was not able to make my change of one dollar and fourteen cents. I became somewhat impatient and told him how much change I was to get, took my food and my change, and left. I was glad this was not a busy time of the day for them.

Even adults don't seem to spend time solving complex problems. They crank up the old computer and it balances their check book for them, or they spend a phenomenal amount of money on a computer program that will baby-sit the kids so they don't have to take the time to solve the problems involved with raising those kids.

We could all be better horsemen and better people if we spent time working on lasting solutions to problems instead of reaching for a quick-fix gimmick. Instead of trying to figure out how to make your horse do something, try putting your ego in a box in the basement and think about how to ask your horse to do it in a way he can understand. See if you can figure out for yourself how to communicate your wishes to your horse using nothing but your hands, arms, legs, and feet.

Large horse ranches raise horses as a business for competition on the cutting, roping, and reining circuits. This requires consideration of the economic factors when getting a horse trained. These events have a three-year-old futurity and the horses entered have about twenty months to get ready to compete. I am in no way discounting the importance of these futurities because they are what determines the monetary value of our horse market. It is not the amount of money awarded to the owner of the winning stallion or filly, but the prestige that goes with winning will set the breeding standards for the coming years. These futurities encourage better breeding practices geared towards improving bloodlines, conformation, and physical and mental ability, which results in the great qualities we find in many of the horses today.

However, the majority of owners do not fall into this category. While you may not have a direct impact on the monetary value of the horse market, you do have an impact on the standards and training methods used. Over seventy-five percent of horse owners do not know how or when to apply any of the training devices on the market. Nor are most of them able to come up with a valid reason to use them.

A very large portion of that seventy-five percent are first-time horse owners; many are first-time riders. I believe in first-timers and admire them for their tenacity and for trying new things. Most of those with whom I have worked have been very receptive to my ideas and appreciative of the knowledge and wisdom I have to offer. It keeps them from having to attend that same school of hard knocks I went to. They also seem to appreciate the fact that I have never forgotten this old-timer was once a first-timer, too.

Whether you are a novice or an experienced horse person give yourself the opportunity to be the best you can be while you are helping your horse be the best he can be. A good horseman has the ability to think. He doesn't want to use anything that takes that ability away from him. A horseman who can't think doesn't have the ability to get his horse to think either. I don't use tie downs, martingales, or any of those things on my horse. Not because I am such a great horseman that I don't need them, but because I strive to be a great horseman with that sense of timing and feel I have observed in those I considered to be great horsemen. I don't want to use anything on my horse that will take away my ability to reason my way through a request. I want to know what the horse needs to do before I ask him to do it and I want to be able to feel when my horse responds properly to my request. If I need my horse to soften in the poll, I want to be able to ask him with a simple snaffle bit, a hackamore, or even a halter. I want to have him respond without forcing him to do it, and I want to be able to feel when he give me the tiniest response so I can develop the timing I need to be able to release the pressure on him immediately.

Keep in mind the two most important training leverages a good horseman can use to get the most from his horse are timing and feel. These things cannot be taught to you by me or anyone else. They are developed over time through experience, and I can't teach you that either. Experience comes from making mistakes, correcting them and learning from them. Experience is the product of working to turn failures into successes.

Timing and feel are an important aspect of becoming a horseman because horses think in milliseconds. When you ask your horse for a response, you have to be able to feel when he has given it to you and your timing needs to be good enough to release the pressure immediately. Otherwise what you are trying to teach him means nothing. If you think about it, the best device for training your horse, for developing timing and feel, and the only one you should really ever need is right at the end of your arms. It's your own hands. Try relying more on your natural training devices and less on the artificial ones.

The horse's desire to be comfortable and find a place in his life where there is zero pressure are the two aspects of the horse's character I use to my advantage. Making the wrong thing uncomfortable by applying physical or mental pressure does not involve inflicting pain or making the horse afraid. I think some trainers confuse respect and fear. Remember, in an earlier chapter I said that fear will make a horse respond but it doesn't teach him anything. A horse that is afraid of you will never respect you. A fearful horse has only one thing on his mind and that is saving his own life. Without respect and trust for you as his protector, a fearful horse is likely to hurt you in an effort to save his life.

HOW TO FIND A GOOD HORSEMAN

There are some good reputable horsemen out there who train horses. I urge you to seek them out. Don't send your horse to a trainer because he is cheap; most good ones aren't. Don't send your horse to a trainer because he drives a fancy, expensive truck and pulls an eight horse, slant-load, full-living-quarters trailer behind it. Talk to the owners of horses he or she has trained. Check out the methods used by the trainer and ask questions. The good ones will work with your horse and help you learn how to work with your horse, too. The good ones recognize that horses are individuals and that most are talented to some degree. Good horsemen adapt to the personality of the horse and know what to do with one that is timid, aggressive, or that has been abused. They know how to design a program to fit the horse because they understand the horse structurally, physically and mentally, and consider all these factors in the design of a program. A good horseman appreciates all horses, even the so-called bad ones, because he understands that it is the bad ones that teach him what it takes to be a good horseman. Anyone, even a bad rider, can ride a good horse. But you have to be a good rider to ride a bad horse. A good horseman helps his horse find that one thing he does best and develops that talent to the greatest degree possible while making as much improvement as he can to all the other areas.

Here are a few additional things you might consider to make sure your horse is going to a place that is good for him. What kind of caretaker is the trainer? Does he have a pasture full of underfed, thin horses? It would be bad enough for your horse to come back untrained, but he doesn't have to come back poor, too. Check out the facility. What kind of conditioning program do they use? Are the stalls adequate? What kind of feeling do you get when you walk in the barn? Is it a depressing place or does it seem to be a lively one with adequate light and ventilation? Is there a minimum amount of dust in the barn or will you have to deal with respiratory problems? What kind of fences are used? Can your horse see them and are they in good shape? Are multiple hazards such as hay forks or old pieces of tin or wire lying about the premises? How many horses are in the barn? If there are none, find out why. If there are more than ten, find out if there is adequate help to care for your horse. Find out if the trainer will be the one to ride your horse or if he has a designee to do that. Is it worth as much money to you to have the horse trained by the designee as it would be to have him trained by the trainer? Is the horse going to be trained in a way that will enable you to ride him when his training is complete? If it is the trainer's bragging that got your attention, is he bragging about how fast his horses are trained or how well he trains them? I don't believe it is possible to train quickly and well.

If I can help people learn to become better horsemen, then I can achieve my goal of improving the quality of life for horses everywhere. In doing so, I also hope to give you a more solid appreciation of the traditional values that formed this country and to rekindle the belief that, even though we sometimes lose our way in this fast paced world, we are really only a quick dusting off from rediscovering and restoring these values into our daily lives.

I want to bring horse training ideas down to a simple concept. When I take a ride into the woods I look at the rocks and the plants and take note of all the little things. Then, if I get lost or turned around, I have all these individual points to help guide me back. Working with your horse is very similar. Really see your horse and note every little thing about him. Learn to recognize when something is wrong with him because you know what is right. If he becomes lost or confused on your training journey you will then be able to guide him back until he reaches a place where he is again secure and comfortable.

Pet, Slave, or Companion
Which One for Your Horse?

I n 1992 I was downsized as a cowboy from the Oklahoma ranch where I had spent twenty years of my life. I never planned on having to go anywhere else or be anything other than a cowboy, and I knew exactly where on the ranch I wanted to be buried when I died. I had used my Teaching by Asking technique with a measure of success on the ranch horses, but I did not know if I could refine the technique enough to teach it to other people. I did not want to be anything other than a cowboy. I was still a cowboy, but now I was an out-of-work cowboy.

Confronted with having to begin my life again at fifty years of age, I drew on my new-found strength, a more solid belief in myself and my talents, and forty-plus years of observing, working with and managing working horse programs. Out of that I built a new and more successful life as the owner of my own full-scale equine consulting service. My life is no longer just about starting young horses on the right path to learning; it is about teaching people how to establish and maintain good solid working relationships with their horses.

One cannot be a successful horse owner without understanding how to maintain a healthy relationship with and care for your equine friend physically and mentally. Knowing horses as I do has given me the ability to teach people how to continue the relationship in a manner that is beneficial to both the horse and the owner at all levels. I now build complete programs, from pre-purchase evaluation for the first-time horse buyer to effective pasture management for working horse and cattle ranches. I construct safety programs for a wide variety of horse operations from local 4-H organizations to feed-lot operations in the west. While my greatest pleasure is and will always be working directly with horses, in order to make a difference in the horses' quality of life, I first have to teach people how to be more effective with horses.

When I speak about improving the quality of life for a horse, I do not mean inviting him into my living room to enjoy the air conditioning and a glass of lemonade on a hot summer day. I do not mean keeping him in a stall

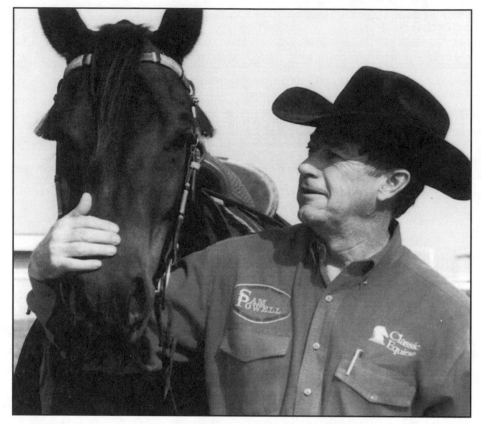

Rooster is my friend, my companion, and my partner, but he is not my pet.

twenty-three hours a day because that stall is safe, warm and dry and I think he should want to be in it. I mean appreciating the horses' culture and way of life, trying to learn as much as I can about them just as they are, and allowing them that culture without thinking it needs to be changed. Human attempts to change the horses' culture create far more problems than they will ever solve.

YOUR HORSE DOES NOT WANT TO BE A PET

In Chapter One we discussed that the horse has a culture of his own and he depends on the dominant member of the herd to help him cope with life's trials and tribulations. A lot of well-meaning horse people create new problems for their horses because they fail to grasp the concept of the horse culture as a culture made up of prey animals and they unknowingly make pets out of them. They expect the horse to behave in the same manner as their dogs or cats because they love on them and pet them and do all sorts of other things the horse does not understand. I am thrilled that horses are included in the category of companion animals along with dogs and cats. They can be wonderful companions. Consider, however, the one thing that makes the horse different from a dog or cat besides his massive size, and that accounts for your horse not responding to you like those other animals. Dogs and cats are predators, just like people. Horses are prey animals. You can't expect the same thing from a horse that you can from a dog or a cat. It is not fair to the horse. You can't change the fact that he is a prey animal; you can adapt to it, however, and you can help your horse overcome his natural fear of predators, but not by making him a pet.

Despite all their wonderful qualities and magnificent beauty, horses do not make good pets. Pets get to ride around in the car and drool on the seat. The neighbor's Blue Heeler dog riding around in the back of the pickup truck is a pet, as are all the cute, cuddly little creatures the kids bring home from school in their backpacks. But 1,200-pound members of the equine culture are not pets. My big, gentle gelding, Rooster, is much better behaved and better mannered than my Border Collie, Darcy. He is my friend, my partner, and my companion, but he is not my pet.

The horse's nature as a prey animal and his cultural upbringing make being a pet nonconducive to his survival. It is confusing to him and it puts the person making the pet of him in potentially grave danger. Keep in mind the horse's natural, instinctive understanding of the pecking order. That is a survival mechanism to him. If you fail to understand his culture as a prey animal and treat him like a big pet, it is similar to thinking of children as "little adults." You treat Horse the same as you would any of your other pets. You walk into his stall to halter him and he rubs his big gentle face all over your new white shirt and you think he really loves you and wants to cuddle, so you cuddle. In reality, Horse is checking out the pecking order in this new herd of two.

Let's look at things from the horse's point of view. Instinct tells him to establish a pecking order in this herd of two and find out where his place is in it. That way he will know exactly what are his duties and responsibilities. He instinctively needs to know whether he has the responsibility of being the whistle blower when danger approaches or whether this other strange-looking member of the herd will take care of that while he takes care of just being a horse.

He turns his rump to you and you scratch it. He walks into your space and rubs and pushes you all around the stall and you pet and coo. He nibbles on your coat sleeve and you kiss him on the nose because you truly believe he is being affectionate. The horse has done all the things he knows to do to establish himself at the top of the pecking order and he has not been scolded, kicked, bitten, sent to his room, or anything else unpleasant. Therefore he instinctively thinks, "I guess this makes me the number one hog at the trough," and he will act accordingly.

Your horse doesn't really want this stately position because he can't relax and be dependent on someone else to stand guard against the predators. The responsibility falls to him and he wonders, "If I get in trouble now, who's going to help me?" By not understanding what is going on in the mind of the horse and by falling in love with those big, soft eyes and wanting to hug your horse all over, you actually take his security away from him.

I have seen declawed domestic house cats attempt to sharpen claws they no longer have because their instinct tells them they must. Your horse will attempt to establish a pecking order, regardless of how insignificant it may seem to you, because his instinct tells him he must. This is most obvious when you have introduced a new horse to an established herd—even if the only other member of that herd is you.

Now that you have unknowingly allowed Horse to establish himself at the top of the pecking order, there comes the time you want to ride Horse away from the barn, just the two of you, with nothing for miles and miles but more miles and miles. You saddle up, lead Horse out, step into the saddle, and head for the pasture gate. But Horse has other plans. He rears up, whirls around, grabs the bit in his teeth, and takes you back to the barn so fast your hat brim rolls back and your eyes water. You wonder what's gotten into your crazy horse. Horse is thinking, "I'm not going out there with no one to protect me. I'm going back to the barn where I know I'll be safe."

A little communication breakdown between two well-meaning members of completely different cultures gives you all the ingredients for a potentially dangerous situation. Awhile back as I was reading one of my favorite western novels, I found a passage that sums up my point. One cowboy, talking about his saddle partner, said, "With my partner by my side I would not be afraid to charge hell with a bucket of water." That is the attitude your horse needs to have about you. That is the attitude he wants to have about you. He needs to be your partner, your companion, and your friend, but not your pet and not your slave. He needs to be confident you will protect him. He needs to feel that he can go into that strange arena or that unknown creek because he has someone to take care of him, to watch for danger and to alert him to that danger in time to escape unharmed.

By making a pet of your horse, though your intentions may be quite good and you physically take wonderful care of him, you actually create some mental problems for him and subject him to a life of confusion. If you expect your horse to work with you and for you to the best of his ability, you must be straightforward with him at all times. Making a pet of your horse sends him mixed signals and then, when it comes down to what you really expect from him, he will be confused and unsure as to how he should behave.

Making the distinction between pet and companion can be difficult for the well-intentioned horse owner. You want your horse to love you and to come running to greet you when you get to the barn. But your lack of knowledge about the equine culture causes you to excuse bad or dangerous behavior and often unknowingly contribute to it. This will result in problems that you will have to deal with farther down the road. If you want to make a pet of your horse, by all means do, but then don't complain because he is not your companion. He can't be both. It is too confusing for him. You

I take things slow and easy when slipping the rope over the colt's head. His progress is measured in the minutest degree.

should also then be responsible enough to realize and accept the liabilities that go along with having a pet that size.

The horses I work with usually tell me what I need to know in order to help them. Often what they tell me is not even close to what the owner is telling me about the problem. Most often what the horses tell me is that their owners haven't been listening while the horse was talking. Listening seems to be a forgotten art these days. I have noticed at my clinics that when people ask questions, before I have had a chance to answer, they're off in an entirely different conversational direction. No wonder there are so many confused horses out there. These people don't take the time to listen to me, so why would I think they have been listening to their horses? Occasionally they'll pretend they're listening to my answer, and then they'll challenge it with, "Yes, but . . . " or "Well we tried that but . . . ." Regardless of the reasons they verbally give me that whatever I suggested they try did not work, I hear every word they are not saying. Sometimes they're saying that Horse did not want to do that so they stopped asking, but more often they're saying that they do not know how to ask Horse to do that so he doesn't do it.

97

Sam demonstrates how to get ahorse to "bridle up."

Horse language is not difficult to understand but you do need to make an effort. If you don't know how to talk to your horse, you won't be able to listen to him either. I can usually tell the people who don't listen to their horses. They are the same ones who don't listen to me. They are also usually the people who have the spoiled, pet horses and who think they have the perfect horses.

During the summer of 1997, I did a series of clinics across the state of Tennessee. Each of the five horsemanship clinics consisted of some thirty kids with their horses, less than one-third of whom actually wanted to be there. One young girl even went so far as to tell me that she was only there because her mom had insisted . . . strongly. However, I could tell who wanted to be there and who didn't without being told. The kids who wanted to be there paid attention and learned something.

One young man was having quite a bit of trouble with his horse. In fact, he got bucked off in front of a lot of people. Nevertheless, he seemed determined to find a way to communicate with his horse. My assistant and I worked with the boy and his horse and over the course of the afternoon he made tremendous progress. Later I visited with his parents. They felt I had been able to help them all to better understand the mind of the horse. That one child wanting to be there more than made up for all the others who did not want to be.

About a month later I received a letter from the boy's father thanking me for helping his boy at the clinic. He went on to tell me about an encounter he had with a skunk that wandered into the garage one night shortly after the clinic. It seems the skunk had every intention of bedding down for the night in the man's garage. The man had other ideas and, having attended a Sam Powell clinic, he felt he ought to be able to get a skunk to move his feet. So, every time the skunk made a move anywhere other than towards the door of the garage, the man started smooching to him. Within five minutes, the skunk was out of the garage, the man was in, and everyone was happy.

This man had listened to what I'd said, and he found a bit of information he was later able to use in a different situation. I am sure he has been just as successful at applying the technique to his horse as he was at applying it to the skunk. Learning to listen to your horse is the first step you should make towards helping your horse become a more respectful, willing partner and companion rather than the disrespectful, dangerous nuisance that pet horses tend to become.

Sadly, in this world, there are people who abuse animals, children, and each other deliberately. Unfortunately, there are also those people who abuse them through ignorance. The number of horses I have seen abused as a result of deliberate cruelty represents a far smaller percentage than those that are abused as a result of ignorance on the part of their owners. Abuse through ignorance, though more obscure, is no less abuse than if it is premeditated.

During one of my many visits to my favorite orthopedic doctor to have my broken leg set after I was kicked by a horse, the doctor asked whether or not the horse had done it on purpose. I asked him if it really mattered. Whether my leg had been broken as the result of an accident or malice on the part of the horse was really not the issue. The end result was the same. So it is with abuse.

My wife is a licensed paramedic by trade, but as a means of reducing the job-related stress associated with her profession she has worked a great deal on the side as a veterinary technician. She has told me many stories of animals, especially grossly overweight dogs, being killed with kindness by well-meaning owners who probably love them very much and will grieve terribly for them when they are gone. Because these owners love their pets, they feed them from the table. They feed the wrong food, at the wrong time, or they just plain feed too much. Killing your horse with kindness is not usually done by overfeeding, (although it is a problem in a few cases) but by making a pet of him. A pet horse is a spoiled horse and a spoiled horse is dangerous. He has no respect for you or anyone else. These horses push on you, bite you, and are more likely to hurt you. Once that happens, the horse gets a reputation and carries a label with him for the rest of his life, however short it may be. He may be sold to another person who is ultimately no more knowledgeable about his culture than the previous owner. He may be sent to a trainer who creates new problems through the use of harsh training methods, gimmicks, or deliberate cruelty. Finally, he may be sent to the killer market to end up as dog food (which this owner can now use to kindly kill his dog through overfeeding).

SOME HORSES CAN'T BE TRAINED

I want you to understand that as much as I love and appreciate the horses in the world I have had to come to the painful realization that there are some horses out there that cannot be helped. Just as there are truly evil people in the world who can not be rehabilitated, so are there horses that can't be rehabilitated. Whether through some genetic flaw or a chemical imbalance in the brain, some horses are born evil. These horses have only one thing on what mind they have—to hurt you. No amount of love and kindness will help. No amount of money spent on the best trainer in the world will help these horses. These horses belong at the killer's. They need to find their place in the dog food can. If you can't see the bad as well as the good then you aren't seeing truth. People who spend time and money on horses like this do a great disservice to themselves as owners, to the trainers hired to work with these horses, and to the many good horses that need homes and kind owners. There will always be trainers who will be more than happy to take your money for as long as you want to spend it and who will keep telling you exactly what you want to hear. But, there are horses out there that are already exactly what you are looking for if you will just take the time to find them. If you have a choice between buying a good horse or trying to make a good horse out of a bad horse, save yourself time, money, heartache, and broken bones by going for the good one. You might even save your life.

When I talk about bad horses like this, I am not talking about the horses that have hurt their owners as a result of the owners' ignorance. I am not talking about horses that have man-made problems because of people's inability to understand and communicate with them. I am not necessarily talking about the horses that were born good and made bad. Most of those can be helped to some degree. I am talking about that one horse out of thousands that should have never been born to start with. Such horses do exist, and you need to be aware of it. I could not consider myself much of a horseman if I led you to believe that any horse can learn to do anything. The first requirement is that he has a mind to work with. Find your horse's place and then help him get to it. You'll both benefit from the effort.

YOUR HORSE IS NOT YOUR SLAVE

As I said earlier, what I do is not so much about helping people with their horses as it is about helping horses with their people. I have to figure out ways to help horses that have people who don't know there's a problem. Sometimes they know there's a problem, but they think they can fix it by bullying and badgering the horse. My work with horses has taught me to use tact and diplomacy instead of force.

Recently, I took my wife to a beautiful place up on the Cumberland Plateau where we trail ride quite often. We went up to spend the day with some friends, so we did not take our horses. We sat in the campground for several hours and watched people come and go on their horses. Late in the afternoon a beautiful sorrel gelding came in carrying his rider, who was so drunk he could barely stay in the saddle. The horse was overheated, but very well-behaved. I watched the rider dismount, tighten the cinch up, remount, and proceed to lope off through the campground.

In a few minutes he loped back past us in the opposite direction and then back again, at which time I saw the rider lean forward in the saddle and smack the horse on the side of the head. He continued loping the horse off a few strides, pulling him up, smacking him and loping him off again. By now the horse was extremely overheated, horribly confused, and in danger of "tying up." I could not figure out what the man was trying to do and neither could the horse, but he kept on trying. I watched for almost an hour thinking that any moment the rider would dismount, stagger back to his campsite, pass out, and that would be the end of it. I even hoped the horse would get his fill and pitch the rider.

Eventually, I realized that the horse would either tie up or collapse before either of those things happened. I was so angry I was shaking, and hiding out and waiting for the situation to go away was not the answer. Charging into the man's camp and beating the hell out of him was not the answer, either. Instead, rather than jerking him off his horse and beating him to within an inch of his life like I wanted to, I mustered up all the tact I have ever possessed and told him what a truly fine horse he had. I told him I was a professional admirer of fine horses and I thought he had one of the finest I had seen in these parts, which was not a lie. I then went on to explain to him that his horse had gotten a little overheated and appeared to be in danger of tying up. I thought it would be a shame if that happened to so fine an animal.

Somewhat alarmed, he asked me what he should do. I told him the horse needed to be cooled out slowly and because his wife was a bit lighter than he, it would be a good idea for his wife to conduct the cooling-out process by walking him down. He agreed and turned the horse over to her while he went off to find another beer. I told his wife that the horse did not need to be ridden at all but hand walked until he cooled down completely. She walked him for quite a while before bedding him down for the night.

I could have gone tearing into that man's camp and inflicted great bodily harm upon him. I was certainly angry enough, but that would have ultimately resulted in this man taking his anger at me out on his horse as soon as he was able. The horse would have gone from being abused as a result of ignorance to being abused as a result of deliberate cruelty, and the end result would have been the same. Being diplomatic about the situation helped everyone come out a winner. The horse got the relief he needed. I got to see a bad situation end before permanent damage was done to the horse. The man got a boost to his ego through my praise and admiration of his horse.

This man's horse was not a pet, but he was not much of a companion either. This horse fell into the slave category. These are horses that no matter what they do, no matter how well they do it, it's not good enough. These horses perform, and keep on performing, out of fear. They will submit time after time, but the owner will never get one hundred percent of the horse's ability because the performance is not done willingly.

The owners who treat their horses this way may get a lot of satisfaction knowing they have made their horse do something, but they never know when the horse will get tired of it, break loose, and rebel. It may never happen, but you can't count on that. When they do rebel, I hope it is not someplace like on the Cumberland Plateau with a 250-foot drop-off real handy.

Making a pet of your horse and making him afraid of you will have similar results in the long run. They can cause you to be injured and subject your horse to a life of confusion and unhappiness. Think about human relationships that are based on mutual respect and trust. The people you are willing to do anything for are usually the ones for which you have the most respect. You don't have a lot of respect for people who push you around, walk all over you, or abuse you. If you will learn the differences that constitute pet, slave, or companion from the horse's point of view, you can save yourself a lot of time, money, and aggravation.

YOUR HORSE CAN BE YOUR COMPANION

As a responsible horse owner, you owe it to your horse to walk that fine line between what makes you comfortable and what makes the horse comfortable. You need to be able to be able to interpret his every move, gesture, and psychological ploy. Your horse deserves to be your companion, not your pet, and not your slave. Remember: while you may not always be in a teaching mode, your horse is always in a learning mode, so be careful how you teach him. He will probably learn the bad things faster than he will the good things, so be careful what you teach him. That way he won't need to go back and unlearn something you never intended him to learn in the first place. Remember that your horse can hear what you don't say even better than I can. Once bad habits take root, your horse won't even think about them. It will not matter if the bad habit has its roots in your ignorance or your cruelty—the end result will be the same. Your horse's actions will always speak louder than your words.

Troubleshooting
Eliminating the Cause of the Problem

The seemingly simple change in my perception of the horse from a dumb animal that needs to be defeated to an animal with a well-structured culture with wants, needs and a desire to be comfortable led to many other physical, mental, and spiritual transformations in my life. I came to realize that many of the difficulties I had encountered during my younger years were the result of my ego-oriented perception of the world. Understanding this led me to a way of permanently correcting a problem by eliminating the cause.

In the garden of everyone's life there will invariably be weeds that, if left to their own accord, will eventually choke the productive life out of the garden. Chopped off at the surface these weeds lie in wait for the proper conditions to bring them forth again and again. But the elimination of those weeds at their source, the root, results in their complete and permanent eradication. This little analogy can be applied to any problem you are having, whether the problem is with your horse, your mate, or your garden.

When you work with horses, whether as a profession or a hobby, you will invariably run into obstacles that will slow your progress. I want you to have a good solid foundation that is based on true knowledge and a complete understanding of the horse so that you will be able to put yourself in all four of his shoes at any given time, perceive the world and the situation as he does, and then figure out how to remove that obstacle.

Thinking like a horse will help you eliminate those obstacles. I don't want you to find a way around the obstacle or even a way over it. If you do, you will spend a lot of time and energy going around or over that same obstacle time after time after time. I want you to be able to stop your horse, dismount, walk over and chunk the obstacle in the ditch so you never have to deal with that same one again. There will be plenty of new ones for you to contend with throughout your journey, so why not eliminate them as you go?

I can't give you a step-by-step, play-by-play means of eliminating the cause of every problem you have, but I can give you some insight as to what goes on in the mind of the horse and how he sees things. Then you will be able to understand why you are having the problem in the first place. Realizing where the problem originates will tell you a great deal about eliminating the cause and thereby the problem.

This chapter will address some of the more common problems I see horse owners attempting to deal with on a day-to-day basis. If you have read this far you are well on your way to developing a better understanding of the mind and nature of your equine, and you will be able to relate to the techniques described here without judging them before you try them.

Remember to think about how the horse sees things through the eyes of a prey animal with survival as his number one goal. He doesn't want to put himself in any situation that will decrease his chance of escape from what he perceives to be a dangerous situation. Then, think about how you previously might have presented the solution to the problem to your horse. I'll bet that your presentation was based purely on a human point of view, and chances are it made the problem worse. Try the following techniques for yourself. I have used each one of them on countless occasions. All that is required in order to get them to work in your favor is understanding of the philosophy behind the technique and having enough patience to see the task through to completion.

Many horse books take a very complicated approach to a relatively simple problem. I am not saying these approaches do not work; I am saying that the teachers do not make the lesson easy enough for the average student to understand and apply. It's like being handed a book on quantum physics by your math teacher because you're having a problem adding 192 and 127. You're pretty sure the book somehow pertains to your problem but you can't comprehend it enough to figure it out. Feeling not only confused about the situation, but also stupid because of your confusion, often compounds the problem.

I believe that the reason there are so many horse books on the market designed to help people work with their horses but still so many people who can't do this is that the authors offer solutions from a human point of view. They write as though the horse already knows what to do. I want to arm you with enough information to understand why you have the problem to start with and then give you the means through which, by thinking like a horse, you can approach the problem from the horse's point of view.

THE DIFFICULT-TO-CATCH HORSE

Perhaps the greatest source of discontent among horse owners everywhere is the horse that cannot be caught. A horse you can't catch is even worse than a horse that will not load (it is certain that I can't load him if I can't catch him). If I could collect the entry fees I have forfeited because of horses I could not catch, I could probably retire and travel around the world.

The difficult-to-catch horse can be a great source of entertainment for those who are watching, but he is a great source of embarrassment and ulcers for the catcher. Little do you realize that your anger only serves to make the situation worse.

I have seen people attempt to bribe a horse into being caught with treats. The problem is that they usually have to give the horse the treats to get close enough to even attempt to catch him. When the treats are all gone, so is the horse. Some people try to sneak up on their horses to catch them, but I have never seen this work either.

A well-meaning friend of my wife's told her that in order to catch her mare she should go and borrow a horse that could be caught and put that horse in the pasture with the mare. My wife thought it a novel idea and borrowed a "catchable" horse from a friend. After a day or two, what she now had were two horses that she couldn't catch instead of one. Whenever she approached the catchable horse, her mare would kick or bite him and send him to the other side of the pasture. Before long the other horse associated the appearance of my wife with the terrible things the mare did to him and he, too, refused to let my wife come near.

There are people who think they can catch their horse by running faster or longer than he can. However, horses can run up to thirty miles per hour for short distances and at slower speeds for much longer periods. Then there is the age-old trick of hiding the halter in the bucket of feed or behind your back when you go out to catch your horse. The idea is that when the horse sticks his head in the bucket for a bite, you slip the halter over his head while he is not looking and he's caught. The problem is that you are not that fast and horses aren't that dumb. You can't put a halter on a horse without him seeing it and a horse that doesn't want to be caught will be off to the back side of the pasture no matter what you have in the bucket. The horse has only to decide whether he wants to eat more than he wants to avoid being caught. If he wants to eat, then hiding that halter has nothing to do with being able to catch him. The only time I have ever seen this technique work was when the horse simply wanted what was in your bucket enough to allow himself to be caught to get it.

Probably the most frustrating situation you can find yourself in with a horse that doesn't want to be caught is when Horse leads you all around the pasture by an invisible lead rope attached to something other than your brain. You approach Horse in the pasture and he lets you get almost close enough to touch him before wandering off a few steps to a new grazing spot. You approach him again. Your fingertips barely brush across his coat and without looking up or missing a single bite, he wanders just out of reach again. Each time you begin your approach you think this time he will stop all the foolishness, stand there and allow you to halter him.

As the sun starts to set in the west, you realize you have wasted the entire day trying to catch that stupid Horse. There is no time to ride, you are no closer to catching Horse than you were when you started, and your thoughts turn to something like, "I'm going to kill you." As soon as Horse hears that thought, he allows you to get only thirty feet from him instead of two. Horse has gotten to walk and graze all day, but you have elevated your stress level, doubled your blood pressure, and fretted ten years off your life.

Horses can be a lot like children. As long as what they are doing is their idea, they want to do it, and if it is something you don't want them to do, they'll do it all day long. The minute you decide to go along with the program, they don't want to do it nearly as much. So, try taking a different approach.

First, get a pocketful of rocks and head for his pasture. (Don't try this an hour before you are due at the horse show.) When you approach Horse in the pasture, if he decides he'd rather run, let him run. Help him run. Start throwing rocks at him. I don't mean pound him with the biggest boulders you can find, but just encourage him to move his feet. If the horse previously led you around a ten-acre pasture with that invisible lead rope, you do the same thing. Make him move his feet. If he gets to decide to move his feet, you get to decide how fast. Send him to the back side of the pasture. When you get to the back side of the pasture, if he wants to go to the front side of the pasture, send him to the front side of the pasture, and quickly. Don't give him much opportunity to air up.

You will discover that Horse won't want to go all over that pasture if it is your idea and not his. When he stops running and allows you to approach, get within a few feet of him and then turn and walk away a few steps. Walk back to him again, watching for signs that he might run. If he runs, help him run. If he stands, approach him and give him a gentle pat or rub on the neck and walk away. At this point, you should either be able to go back and halter Horse or go on back to the barn with him following you. You may have to send him to the other side of the pasture three or four times, but if you will turn your back and walk away from him each time he stops and looks at you and then reward him for standing there, it will be worthwhile in the long run. If you continue this process for a few days, you will no longer have a horse that you can't catch.

Many people make the mistake of only catching their horse when they want to do something. In most cases it involves something pleasurable for the rider and hard work for the horse. In this case the horse may go sour on being caught and want no part of it. You can apply this same technique, but it may take longer if the horse is really soured. The best thing you can do to keep this from happening is visit him occasionally when you don't want anything from him. Take your halter out and put it on him and rub him and take it right back off. Take your halter with you and rub your horse with it without putting it on him at all. Then go back to the barn. Don't make your horse dread seeing you coming across the pasture because he knows he is going to have to go someplace where he is not comfortable. If you vary your routine so Horse doesn't know what to expect and make life comfortable for him, you will never again have to forfeit another entry fee because you can't catch your horse.

Always be aware of your feelings and attitude when you go to catch your horse. He can sense hostility. If there is a horse that you absolutely hate and you think about how much you hate that horse while you are trying to catch yours, you will have a great deal of difficulty. Your horse simply senses your hostility. He has no way of knowing that he is not the cause of it. He just wants to keep himself safe by staying out of range of the hostility you are emanating.

THE DIFFICULT-TO-LOAD HORSE

Another common source of frustration and aggravation for the horse owner comes from the horse that will not load. What can start out as a case of simple frustration over a forfeited entry fee at the horse show can quickly turn to tragedy and heartbreak when the horse that will not load needs to be taken to the veterinarian's office. For these reasons, if no other, I make sure that trailer loading is a part of my training program.

People may not realize what constitutes a difficult-to-load horse. If you feel as though you have to pick the horse's feet up and place them in the trailer and then get around behind and give him a boost, you have a difficult-to-load horse. If you have to gather all the neighbors within a one-mile radius and warn them to pack a lunch because they're coming to help you

I start teaching a horse to load by backing the trailer up to the pen. Horse owned by Glenn Oaks Farm.

The first thing you have to do when teaching the horse to load is show him there is no danger in the trailer.

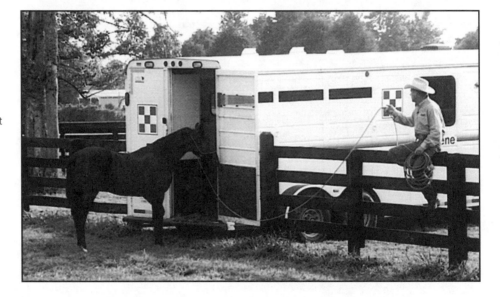

Anytime the horse looks at the trailer, let him think about it for a minute.

load your horse, you have a difficult-to-load horse. In my opinion any horse that loads any way other than quickly, quietly, and willingly needs to be taught to load before he is taught anything else. Horses are not born knowing how to load and unload from a trailer. The horse's instinctive fear of closed-in spaces makes entering a horse trailer an unnatural, and therefore fearful, thing for him to do.

You do not have to accept difficulty in loading your horse as a permanent way of life, contrary to what you may have been told. Before asking a horse to enter a trailer, you must first teach him that there is no danger in there, and you can't lie to him about it. When a horse sticks his head in a

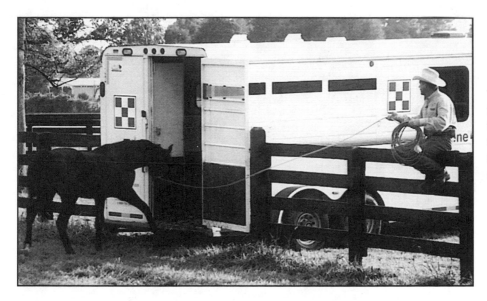

The horse will eventually associate the trailer with a sanctuary, a place to get relief from the discomfort.

trailer he is naturally afraid. While he is standing there trying to figure out whether or not it is a place he wants to be, most people decide to whack him across the rump to hurry him into the trailer. Horse already had some trepidation and all you've done is reinforce his fear. Horse already had in his mind that if he stuck his head in that dark hole something bad was going to happen, and sure enough it did. He felt pain.

I start teaching the horse to load by backing the trailer up to a pen so that the trailer opening is almost flush with the rest of the panels of the pen. I want the trailer to kind of look like part of the pen. The object is to get Horse to move his feet. At first it doesn't matter where he moves them, but you have to make him uncomfortable enough to move them. You can work on directing where he puts them later. You can use Horse's instinctive desire to be comfortable to your advantage in this situation. If he is not comfortable in one place he will find someplace where he is comfortable. I use a war bridle and a sixty-foot rope, but you can get the same results by tossing rocks, dirt clods or even peach pits at his feet. The purpose is not to inflict pain or create fear, but only to make him uncomfortable enough to move his feet. I don't care if he gets mad at this point—I am up on the fence out of his line of fire, and if he is mad he is much more subject to move his feet in search of a comfortable spot away from the aggravation.

Anytime Horse makes a move towards the trailer, or even looks at it in the beginning, I stop irritating him. I remove the physical and mental pressure and allow him to find some comfort. If he walks away from the trailer or locks his feet and refuses to move, I aggravate him some more to make the wrong move uncomfortable. In a few minutes, Horse figures out that he's more comfortable and things are a lot quieter over near that dark hole. The trailer becomes a haven, a sanctuary, rather than something to be afraid of.

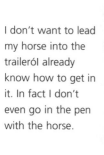
I don't want to lead my horse into the trailer—I already know how to get in it. In fact I don't even go in the pen with the horse.

As I continue to work with him using this technique, Horse comes to the conclusion that the only way to get away from the aggravation is to go and hide in that dark hole. He will walk over and stick his head in or he may hop right in. If he doesn't immediately go in I give him a chance to think about it and figure it out on his own. If he starts to back out, I aggravate him some more. If he just stands there, I aggravate him some more. Timing is important. You must apply the pressure and take it off at the right time. A good rule of thumb is that if you are applying mental pressure and nothing happens, you should apply more. If the horse is moving his feet in the proper direction, you're applying enough. Be willing to apply whatever pressure is needed to get a response. If it takes two ounces, then stop at two ounces, but if you need ten pounds be willing to use that much. If you put a pot of water on the stove to boil and you come back in fifteen minutes to find nothing is happening to the water, the best thing to do is turn the heat up. It is physically impossible for a 150-pound man to make a 1,200-pound horse get into a trailer, but you can make him want to get in it.

I never lead my horse into the trailer. I already know how to get in it. Horse is the one that needs to learn how. When you go into a tight place such as a trailer with a horse, you put yourself in danger of being mashed against the wall of the trailer or stepped on if he gets scared before you get out. Either one can result in injuries that range from very minor to fatal. In fact, when I am teaching a horse to load I don't even go in the pen with him. I create discomfort for him using the war bridle or the dirt clods while I am sitting on the fence rail ten to fifteen feet from the trailer. That way he does not associate his discomfort with anything I am doing.

Some people put hay or grain up in the front of the trailer in an effort

I want the horse to do the thinking and learn how to get in the trailer.

I want the horse to make the decision to get in the trailer because he knows it is the best place for him to be.

to lure their horse in. What they don't realize is that if the horse doesn't want to get in that trailer no amount of feed will make him get in it, and if he does want to get in it then they don't need the hay or grain. Most grown horses can put their front feet in a two-horse side-by-side trailer and reach the feed in the bin without ever getting their back feet in. If that happens you may as well go get the roller skates for his back feet because that is about the only way you'll get that horse down the road. I hay my horses in the trailer on a long road trip, but I put the hay in after the horse is loaded, and not before.

I have seen some people successfully employ the use of buggy whips and butt ropes to get a horse to load. If they work for you and they are not used to inflict pain, I don't object. The principle is supposed to be the same as far as creating discomfort for the horse. My thinking is that I want all of Horse's attention going forward, not backward. I want him studying that trailer, not worrying about something slipping up behind him. He is already suspicious that something might do just that, and I don't want to confirm his suspicion.

I want the horse to do the thinking and learn how to get in the trailer. I want him to look for that trailer anytime he gets scared and to get in that trailer just because the door is open. I want him to get in the trailer based on his knowledge that it is the safest place for him to be.

If you rely on crutches, sooner or later you will find yourself in a situation where you have to load your horse but you have no feed, no whip, no rope, and no one else around to help. Why not invest a little time at the beginning of your program to teach your horse this potentially life-saving lesson? In the long run it will save you a lot of time you could be spending teaching him other fun things. You don't have to think for your horse. He has a brain; you just need to help him use it.

Often people think their horse won't load because the trailer is too high off the ground and he doesn't know how to step that high. The same horse will jump a creek a half-mile wide to keep from getting his feet wet and has no problem picking his feet up enough to step over a fallen tree. He can figure out how to get in that trailer if you set it up for him. The thing is not to crowd him, not to push him beyond his mental limit at any given moment, and not to pull on him. Set it up for him and let him figure it out. He will find the exact spot where he needs to be to get comfortable again if you will allow him to look for it. Always reward him when he finds it by allowing him to be comfortable. If you will take time to teach him right the first time, you won't need to give the lesson again.

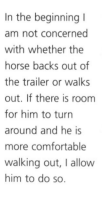

In the beginning I am not concerned with whether the horse backs out of the trailer or walks out. If there is room for him to turn around and he is more comfortable walking out, I allow him to do so.

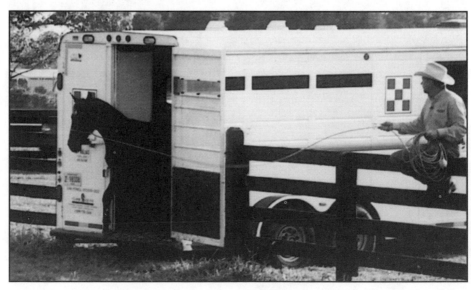

Remember: Don't make a big deal out of loading. If he puts his front feet in the trailer and then runs backwards, just be grateful he has come that far and start the process all over again. It will not take nearly as long for him to run over and put his front feet back in the trailer. If he gets in and then hops right back out, relax and congratulate yourself for having a horse that has taught himself to unload. He will have to know how to do it sooner or later.

One of my clients asked me to help him with his horse because he could not get him to unload from the trailer. He said that his horse had previously backed out of the trailer as soon as the butt bar was lowered, so he started buggy whipping him any time he tried to back out of the trailer. I could understand why the horse would not unload if he was whipped every time he tried it!

In the beginning I am not concerned with whether Horse walks out of the trailer or backs out of it. If there is room in the trailer for him to turn around and he is more comfortable walking out, I allow him to do so. Keep in mind that when your horse is backing out of a trailer, he doesn't know whether it is six inches or sixty feet to the ground. He can't see behind him, so he might be a bit apprehensive if not downright terrified. Allow him to feel his own way through the situation. If he doesn't want to come out of the trailer, use the same technique of making him a little uncomfortable until he does come out. Remember to measure his progress in millimeters and reward him for any effort. It could take two hours or ten minutes, but the lesson he learns is well worth spending however much time it takes for him to learn it.

Nothing I have talked about here involves the use of force applied by any means, fear used to any extent, or pain inflicted to any degree. If you will use your eyes to see the whole horse, watch for any move in the right direction, and reward the horse for making that effort, you will not have to rely on brutality to teach your horse. If he moves a foot, an ear, or even shifts his weight in the direction you want him to go, reward him for that and he will learn what you want him to do much more quickly than he will if you get behind him and start beating on him. Doing that will only make him afraid, confused and difficult, if not impossible, to load, and you will go through this scene every time you want to trailer your horse.

Make that trailer his sanctuary and he will look for it long after the trailer loading lesson is complete. Do everything in your power to make sure your trailer is never a source of pain or discomfort, but a safe place for your horse and you will not have a problem getting him to load.

If you use your trailer once or twice a year and the rest of the year it just sits in the yard, check it out well for wasps and bees before you ask your horse to get into it. If you are in the market to buy a trailer and you find one you like, have a friend pull it around a few miles while you ride in the back before you sign on the dotted line. If it is not comfortable enough for you to ride in, your horse won't want to spend much time in it either. Finally, be cognizant of your driving habits when you are trailering your horse. If you slam on the brakes, make jack-rabbit starts or stand your truck and trailer on two wheels as you take the curves, your horse won't want to load and go anywhere with you. If your horse has become increasingly difficult to load over a period of time, check out these things as possible causes. In the meantime, happy trailer loading.

THE SPOOKY HORSE

Aside from being a source of aggravation and unpleasant rides, a horse that spooks can put his rider at risk of serious injury or even death. Given a choice, I'd rather have a horse that tries to run away instead of buck, but only if he has enough control on him for me to regain control of the situation before anyone gets hurt.

As I said in an earlier chapter, there is no way that you can completely "bomb-proof" a horse. You might get him to stand still and watch ten semi-trucks go by only to be completely undone when the eleventh one goes by blowing an air horn. You can't possibly know from one day to the next, or even minute to minute, what things or situations a horse will perceive as dangerous. Just because he did not spook at the yellow school bus today does not mean he will not spook at that same yellow school bus tomorrow when a little girl waves out the window. You cannot expose a horse to every situation beforehand and know how he will react to that same situation in the future because, for some reason unknown to you, he may not perceive it as the same. Remember the story about the rag in Chapter Four.

What you need to do with a horse that spooks (and with any horse that you plan to spend time with) is install safety valves. Teach him how to stop and turn around, and to do it on cue. Having a solid foundation on your horse automatically gives you safety valves that could save your life or the life of your horse.

If a horse that has been taught to be soft from side to side spooks and starts to buck, you can reach down, take hold of one rein, ask him to give you his face and pull him out of it. If he starts to buck and he has been taught to move forward off your leg pressure, you can use your legs to drive him forward, disengaging his rear end, and drive him out of it. It is anatomically impossible for a horse to buck or rear up if his back end is moving.

If a horse that runs away when he is spooked has been taught to be soft from side to side, you can ask him to give you his face to the side and pull him into a circle that will have to slow him down if you make the circle progressively smaller. If this horse has been taught to stop properly, you should only have to ask him to do so. If you have a problem using any of these things to regain control of a horse that spooks, you have not spent enough time on the basics. His foundation is weak. I urge you to go back and rebuild it solidly before the structure tumbles down on top of you.

If your horse spooks, his first reaction is to flee. He will gather himself up, make a quick turn, and attempt to get out of Dodge. It is important that you keep him facing whatever he is afraid of long enough for him to see that it will not hurt him. If he turns left, you have to turn him back to the right. If he makes a 360-degree turn to the right and comes back to face the object again, you must turn him 360 degrees to the left and get him to face the object. If he makes a complete circle, even though he may still be facing the object, in his mind, he escaped it by his action. Once you get him to come back and face the object, make him to stand there long enough to see that there is no danger and that you will not allow him to be harmed. You can't keep him from being afraid. All you can do is to help the horse learn to control his fear.

If you have not taken the time to install those safety valves and your horse has no control you will not be able to pull his head around with a come-along. Once you put control on your horse, you will be surprised to find that the spooky horse doesn't spook nearly as easily and if he does, it's not a big, scary deal. A frightened, out-of-control horse coupled with a rider who does not know what to do in a panic situation can have deadly consequences. It won't do any good for your horse to know how to turn around if you don't know how to ask him. By the same token, it will not do you any good to ask him to turn around if he doesn't know how to do it. A math teacher can ask a student to divide forty-nine by seven all day long, but if the student hasn't been taught the math basics, that teacher will still be asking him to do it long after the cows come home.

CRIBBING, FIDGETING, STALL WEAVING

These annoying habits generally have their roots in boredom. Many horses are stabled more than they are kept on pasture because they are in competition on the show circuit, because their owners think it's best for them, or because they can't be caught. If I had to spend twenty-four hours a day in a twelve-by-twelve stall, I'd be difficult to catch, too. Horses don't have thumbs to twiddle when they get bored, so they resort to other things. They start to chew on their stalls, or move back and forth (stall weavers). Horses, by nature, are designed to walk and graze. Their evolution as prey animals makes standing in one spot unnatural and uncomfortable. Keeping a horse in a stall and feeding him a high protein feed increases his need for movement and exercise, but because he can't move around much in his stall he gets fidgety or he weaves back and forth (hence the term stall weaver). Nature tells the horse to move so he moves. Such horses never seem to get comfortable and relax because they have too much pent-up energy. Horses that are not allowed to move about and socialize can wind up with all sorts of neurotic behavior.

The annoying and costly habit cribbing also has its roots in boredom. The theory is that the horse gets bored, starts looking for something to do, and starts to chew on his stall. Somewhere in the process the horse tries to pull on the wood between his front teeth, which causes pain. The pain causes a natural reaction of the release of endorphins, the body's naturally-produced painkiller (similar to morphine). It is believed that after a relatively short period of time, the horse becomes addicted to the endorphin release, much the same as humans sometimes become addicted to painkillers after a traumatic injury. In short, the horse becomes a junkie.

Once a horse starts cribbing, it is nearly impossible to stop. People employ the use of a cribbing collar, which is supposed to deter the cribbing action by preventing the horse from tightening his neck muscles enough to pull with his teeth. These collars stop the cribbing action, but fall short of eliminating the horse's desire to do it. Once the collar is removed the horse will go right back to cribbing again. What starts out as a problem with boredom for your horse actually becomes a chemical-dependency problem. The best solution to the problem is to prevent boredom. Don't ever let cribbing get started.

It should be noted here that horses that crib do not necessarily chew, and horses that chew are not all cribbers. Horses that chew do not necessarily become cribbers, but chewing can certainly lead to cribbing further down the road. Most horses that crib are kept up on a continuous basis. There are exceptions to every rule and you should arm yourself with enough knowledge to be able to figure out whether your horse is cribbing or chewing. If he is chewing you need to determine whether he is chewing because he's bored or because he likes the taste of what he's chewing on.

Pay attention to your horse. If you are going to keep a horse in confinement, whether in a twelve-by-twelve-foot stall or a thirty-acre pasture, then accept the responsibility as his caregiver for figuring out what he needs to maintain a healthy mental and physical state. Remember that mental stress will lead to physical problems in the long run for your horse, just as it will for you.

THE HORSE THAT WON'T STAND TIED

During one of the summers I spent with my dad, he suggested I go to a nearby farm to help the old gentleman brand his coming two-year-olds. I was anxious to do anything I could that would help me become a great horseman, so I paid the man a visit and got a job.

The first day I reported for work, the old man had ninety-five colts in a large outdoor arena. He had the fire going and the branding irons ready. I took a look around and assumed the rest of the hired help would be there shortly.

The man rode over to me on his horse and began to explain to me exactly what he wanted me to do, which was simply to place the hot iron on the colt's left hip, count to six, and take it off again. It seemed easy enough, provided the rest of the help arrived soon. The man rode off with his rope in hand in search of the first colt. I could stand it no longer and I asked, "Where's the rest of the help?"

"You're it, Son," he replied.

"Oh, no . . . ," I mumbled to myself.

The old man must have sensed my anxiety because he tried to assure me that I was all the help he would need as he dropped his loop over the first colt's head. I was sure his confidence had to do more with his ability as a horseman than my willingness to get myself killed, and I felt a little better.

He had tied a knot in his rope so that the honda could not slide down far enough to tighten around the colt's neck and cut off his air supply. Once the rope was around the colt's neck, the slack was taken out of it when the colt began to back up. With the slack was gone, the colt just planted his feet. He did not pull back or throw a fit as I was sure he would. He simply stood there while I placed the hot branding iron on his hip for a count of six. Then the man rode over to the colt, removed his rope, and aimed for the next one. By the end of the day we had branded all ninety-five colts and barely stirred up the dust in the arena.

The trick here was to give the colt something to pull on. When he reached the end of the rope, he simply planted his feet and sat back against the tension in it. Because the rope did not tighten up around his neck and cut off his air supply, the colt did not fight it—he just pulled back and stood there. Herein lies the key in teaching a problem horse to stand tied: *Don't* give him anything to pull back on. I will explain.

Countless halters, snaps, and lead ropes have been broken and nearly as many horses have been injured because they have not been taught to stand tied. I don't tie my horses a lot because if something frightens them, their first instinct is to run. If I have taught them well enough to face fear and look for me if they get into trouble, they will be more willing to stand tied but less likely to need to be tied. Usually when my horse is being groomed or shod he is not tied. If he is tied up he can't run if something frightens him, and that is when horses throw fits, break things, hurt you, hurt themselves, and learn how not to stand tied.

Once a horse pulls back on his halter or lead rope out of fear, impatience, or whatever, and breaks it, then it becomes an ongoing quest to find stronger and stronger halters and lead ropes that he can't break. The secret is not to go find something stronger for him to pull back on; it is to not give him anything to pull back on in the first place.

Some trainers tie a horse to an inner tube and let him pull on it. The theory is that the horse will get tired and stop pulling. It is a great theory and it will work. However, the rubber reaches a point where there is no more stretch and at that point the colt has something to pull back on. I have seen an inner tube break, and a horse blinded by it. Always keep your horse's safety in mind.

If you have a horse that will not stand tied, try putting him in a twelve-by-twelve stall with his halter on. I recommend using a thin rope halter with no hardware. Sometimes the metal hardware on the web halters fatigues or is defective and will break easily. Rope halters also put a little more pressure on the horse's poll than the webbed ones. It is more uncomfortable for him to pull in this type of halter.

Take a nylon rope and place it over a rafter in the stall, preferably one right over the perimeter of the stall. Attach the outside end of the rope to a heavy bale of hay. Make sure the twine or wire around the hay bale will not break, or secure it with another piece of nylon rope. Leave just enough length of rope inside the stall to attach to the colt's halter with him standing in a natural position with his head slightly elevated. Attach the nylon rope to his halter. As he begins to pull back the hay bale lifts off the ground, but before he plants his feet and begins to really pull he has reached the far side of his stall and can go no farther. So, he either stands there holding the heavy bale of hay in the air, or he walks back and sets it down again and finds relief from the pressure.

If the nylon rope doesn't slide freely over the rafter, try placing an old nylon cinch over the rafter and run the rope through the D-rings of the cinch. Soon you will be able to tie that horse with a piece of string from a feed sack. He won't know it is not attached to a bale of hay or how far he can pull before he reaches the wall that he is sure is behind him.

When I was teaching my dog, Darcy, to obey the "come" and "stay in here" commands, I placed a section of rope around her neck. When I told her to come I would tug on the rope. Now when we travel she pretty much has free rein to go and do as she pleases because she is so well-behaved. If she gets a little rambunctious I only need to place a very short section of rope around her neck. It doesn't even have to touch the ground. She thinks it's five miles long and I can pull on it whenever I want. I call it her "minding rope" and she is extremely well-behaved when wearing it. This same principle is behind this technique to teach your horse to stand tied.

When you pull on a horse, all you teach him is that he can pull more than you can. I have seen people trying to teach a horse to lead by dragging him behind a tractor. That may teach him to lead, but not willingly, and it doesn't teach the horse to stand tied. If you will use the technique I just described, your horse will tie as securely with a feed sack string as he would with a logging chain because he will not have any idea that he can break whatever he is tied with. All he knows is that whenever he has pulled back it's been really uncomfortable, and it is much more comfortable to just stand there.

Once you have taught your horse to stand tied, tie him frequently. This is a great way to teach him patience. During training, horses that are in my care may not be ridden every day but they are trained every day. Patience is part of their training program. My horses are frequently saddled, tied off, and left while I go do other things. If the horse paws, fidgets, or otherwise lets me know he is not happy, he wants attention. If I walk over and scold him or untie him and take him back to the barn then I have given him exactly what he wanted . . . attention.

When the colt gets quiet and stops making a scene then I will go untie him. He learns that acting up is a lot of work for nothing. It isn't going to accomplish anything except making him tired. If you are pushed for time, watch him continuously and wait for a moment when he gets quiet to go untie him. He will associate what he is doing at that precise moment with what you are doing to him. It only takes releasing him during that quiet moment for him to realize that is what he should do. Soon you will not need to tie him at all.

Horses really want to do things the easy way. Sometimes it is up to you to show them what the easy way is.

HALTER-BREAKING/LEADING

During my lifetime I have been witness to countless methods used to halter-break colts, some of which I thought were comical, while others were down-right dangerous. Man could certainly make his interaction with the horse world a little less imperfect by using his brain and thinking about what he is trying to do.

There are people who put the colt in a stall at about twelve weeks of age and go toe-to-toe with him. They wrestle the colt around the stall and somehow manage to get the halter on, often while the colt is standing on his hind legs pawing with his front feet. The colt has been mentally terrorized, physically traumatized, and even the largest people have been known to come out with some sort of physical trauma, from cuts and bruises to broken bones. Needless to say, this is not a good technique for someone of my wife's stature to use. She is five feet tall and weighs one hundred and ten pounds. I don't think she would fare very well going toe-to-toe with a colt, even if he is only twelve weeks old.

I use the same technique to halter break babies that I use to start an older horse under saddle. I halter-break my babies at sixteen weeks, the same day that I wean them off their mother. Up to that point I don't fool with them. I want them to learn how to be a horse, and the best one to teach them that is their mother.

A lot of behavior is learned, and for that reason if I have a baby on an ill-tempered mare, I may pull the baby off earlier than sixteen weeks—before he's had a chance to learn the mare's bad manners. I won't wean him early enough to jeopardize his health and well-being, but I don't want to start out having to break the bad habits he learned from his mama.

We studied the brood mares on the ranch where I worked in Oklahoma. The mares that were ill-tempered and had bad habits such as pinning their ears, avoidance of humans, disrespect, etc., had babies that acted the same way. So we started taking foals off the ill-tempered mares and putting them on surrogate mares that were more even-tempered and better behaved, or we weaned the babies early, or we transferred the embryos from ill-tempered but well-producing mares to even-tempered but not so conformationally perfect recipient mares. We found all these babies to be better behaved and easier to work with.

Halter-breaking colts is the only time I recommend the use of a solid-sided round pen. I take the mama and the baby into the round pen, and then I take the mare back to the pasture, which usually takes about thirty minutes, meanwhile leaving the baby alone in the round pen. Now, this baby has never been alone in his life and he is scared to death. He is looking for someone to take care of him, protect him, and make him comfortable. Basically, I go in and take the place of his mama.

Using my Teaching by Asking technique, I send him away from me in the beginning in order to establish myself at the top of the pecking order. We go through all the steps of the lesson in respect and moving his hip over when I approach. Usually by now the colt is following my every step. Because he is beginning to trust me, he will allow me to ease my rope over his head if I go slowly enough.

I ask him to make a step toward me by applying a little pressure on the rope. If he does not take a step I encourage him a little more to move his feet by taking a step to the side. I compromise with him. I let him know that if he moves his feet I will show him where to put them. I make him a little more uncomfortable by pulling him to one side. I don't take hold of him and drag him all around the pen and I don't keep pulling on the rope so he passes out from lack of oxygen. Teaching a colt to lead requires his cooperation. If you ask him to take a step toward you by applying pressure to the rope and he doesn't, then you only do what is necessary to make him uncomfortable enough to move his feet. When he takes a step, you release the pressure.

This colt has now bonded with you and you have already taught him how to lead with a rope over his head. All that is left is to replace the rope with a halter and lead him to the barn. This is much easier than going at him with the halter in his stall and hoping you can get it on him before he kills you or himself.

Using this technique you have a colt that is halter-broke and knows how to lead. Experience has told me that the two do not necessarily go together. Just because a horse wears a halter does not mean he knows how to lead. Any horse will lead if you can get him to move his feet, but his first instinct when you pull on him is to pull back with twice as much force. Remember, his survival instinct tells him to resist pressure. It does not matter which end you put the pressure on, his first instinct is to resist it. That is why you can achieve better results teaching your colt to lead if you will try untracking him side to side rather than just hauling back on the end of the rope. It gets the colt to move his feet. If you release the pressure at that moment, he will learn that is what you want without anyone making a big deal of it.

If the colt takes a couple of steps and you fail to release the pressure, he will be confused and think that he must not be doing what you want. He'll start looking for another way to find relief from the pressure. Sometimes, the harder the leader leads the faster the horse goes, and the faster the horse goes the harder the leader pulls. Where is the horse's motivation to learn, "Horse this is what I want you to do," if he never finds that point of release?

I have successfully started many colts at my clinics that were not halter-broke and ridden them within the two-hour time frame. However, it is much easier to teach them to lead as weanlings. They have an opportunity to learn more over a longer period of time. Asking a horse to absorb so much knowledge in a two-hour crash course is hard on him. A lot of times I have no horse left mentally at the end of the clinic.

There is a Zen philosophy that that employs the practice of slowing down to go faster. There is no better time to use that philosophy than when you are working with horses. By slowing down and taking time to teach them correctly in the beginning, you save so much time and energy by not having to go back and repeat lessons. You will not spend countless hours fixing mental or physical problems that you created by being in a hurry and pushing your horse beyond his mental and physical capabilities.

LEAD CHANGES

At every single clinic I have held there has been at least one person who asks me to demonstrate a lead change. I don't know if they are trying to learn how to do it themselves or if they are just trying to find out if I can do it. I stopped trying to prove myself to people a long time ago, and the people who ask for this demonstration are usually novice riders or even pre-novice, wannabe horse owners who haven't even enough experience to understand the explanation.

The lead change or flying lead change is something all horses know how to do. Watch your horse in the pasture. If he is running in his right lead and he wants to make a left-hand turn, he will switch over to his left lead in order to make a comfortably balanced turn and reduce his chances of falling.

To determine which lead your horse is in, note which front foot hits the ground first. His back feet should correspond to his front. If they do not, it is known as a cross canter or cross-firing. The horse is in one lead in the front and the opposite lead in the back. This is often a man-made problem and is just as physically uncomfortable for the horse as it is for the rider.

A lead change done in a competitive setting and on cue is an advanced maneuver that should not even be attempted by most of the people who ask me how to do it. There are many things involved with the lead change that you must know prior to asking your horse to do it.

First, the horse has to know how to move away from pressure. Remember basic number three from Chapter Four. If he has not been taught to move off your leg he will not be able to execute a lead change on cue. Second, he will have to know how to pick up either lead on cue from a standstill. He will have to do it consistently and successfully. Third, you will have to know how to ride and how to communicate with your horse so that you can ask for what you want. Fourth, you will have to know how to set him up in the proper anatomical position so he can give you what you want when you ask for it. Fifth, you will need to be cognizant enough to know when he has given you what you asked for. You can only do that by knowing the mechanics involved with the lead change.

When a horse changes leads he changes in the back first. If you want your horse to change leads, get him to move his hip over. If he can't move his hip over he will not be able to complete the lead change and may end up cross-firing. This has nothing to do with training; it has to do with anatomy. However you go about asking your horse to change leads, at some point the request has to involve a cue to move his hip over.

This can be as simple or as complicated as you care to make it, but the end result will be the same. The horse has to move his hip over in order to execute a lead change. People often make it complicated because they don't know enough about what they are asking the horse to do or because they have asked him to do something he has not been taught. All horses know how to change leads, but they have to be taught to change leads on cue.

Use the k.i.s.s. (keep it simple, stupid) principle as much as possible when working with your horse. Don't make anything more difficult or complicated than necessary. Working with him will be a lot more fun and a lot less work. Stop asking your horse to do things that neither of you is ready for and your relationship will be safer and happier.

Commonly Asked Questions

This final chapter addresses some of the questions most frequently asked at my clinics. The answers I give are based on forty-plus years of personal experience working with horses of all breeds and temperaments. They are not meant to, in any way, discredit anyone else who works with horses for a living. They are simply those things that I have tried and found to be successful. They are not the only methods available, nor are they the only methods that work, but the things I have taught you throughout this book have certainly made my job of teaching horses a lot easier on both of us. They are based on simplicity.

HOW CAN I GET MY HORSE TO STAND STILL WHILE I GET ON HIM?

Horses that will not stand still for mounting are not only annoying, but dangerous as well. I don't want my horse to walk off down the trail while I have one foot in the stirrup and my rear higher in the air than my head.

Some people mount their horses with their foot stuck in the stirrup clear to the boot heel. When the horse starts walking the rider jerks on the reins, causing the horse to jump or rear up. The rider has to mount in a hurry because he is unable to get his foot out of the stirrup.

Jerking on the reins does not help the horse understand what you want. He thinks that every time you put your foot in the stirrup his mouth will hurt, so he moves around to keep you from putting your foot in the stirrup and making his mouth hurt. The problem escalates and will only get worse if you do not take corrective action.

First, as you prepare to mount your horse, make sure he is standing squarely on all four feet with his weight evenly distributed. That way, when you put your weight in the stirrup, he will not have to struggle to maintain his balance or move forward a step or two to square himself up. Second, put your foot in the stirrup only as far as the ball of your foot. If your horse walks out from under you or you lose your balance and fall backwards with your foot in the stirrup all the way to your boot heel, the toe of your boot will lodge against the top of the stirrup and you are hung. To put it in cowboy lingo, you are in a world of hurt if that horse runs. If this should ever happen to you and you can maintain your mental capacities long enough to think, try to remember to roll over onto your belly and your foot will find itself free at last. From personal experience, however, this will probably be the fourth or fifth thing that comes to mind after you have slid across the barnyard. You will think about your brains being kicked out and wonder whether your insurance policy is paid up before you think to roll over, so it is best not to put yourself in that predicament.

If you can't reach the stirrup easily, then let it down so you can reach it until you have taught your horse to stand still for mounting. We are working on mounting here, not riding. As soon as you get ready to mount, put your left hand on the horse's neck about halfway up, and your right hand on the cantle of the saddle. This is usually where, without meaning to, we teach our horse to move. Usually you push down on the stirrup while pulling on the horse's neck and the cantle with all your strength in an effort to pull the horse underneath you as you get airborne. I know it sounds stupid, and it looks really bad, too, but I see it all the time.

Instead, as you begin to mount use your hands for balance rather than to pull with. Stand as close to your horse's side as possible and push yourself up with your left leg, just as you would to climb stairs or a ladder. If your horse doesn't move his feet, reward him by sitting down squarely in the saddle. Mounting is not comfortable for the horse because he has to work to maintain his balance. Don't make mounting a long, drawn-out thing—get on up there and sit down.

If your horse starts to move his feet, ease back on the reins a little and keep your weight in the stirrup until he quits moving. Then you can either reward him by getting out of the stirrup and trying again, or you can finish mounting. It is very uncomfortable for him to have you hanging on his side like that, so if he is going to move around, make it as uncomfortable as possible. When he quits moving, sit down and let him be comfortable.

It will not take the horse long to figure out which is best, but you have to help him. Don't add to his misery by poking him in the ribs with the toe of your boot, or try to pull him over while you lumber your way up, or jerk on his mouth.

WHAT ABOUT LEAVING THE HORSE'S HALTER ON AT ALL TIMES?

Everywhere I go I see horses in the pasture wearing halters. The reasons people give for this are things like they can't catch the horse or they just don't want to take the time.

Laziness, impatience, and just-don't-give-a-hoot attitudes on the part of the owners has caused untold suffering to horses. One owner turned several horses wearing halters into a 150-acre pasture. He checked on his horses only on weekends. When one turned up missing he asked me to help him search. We found the horse in the timber where he had caught his halter on a tree limb. From the looks of the ground around the tree, the horse had struggled quite a long time before giving up and just falling down. We found his body hanging from the tree by his halter.

While I was paying a visit to a veterinarian's office in Oklahoma a few years ago, a lady brought her filly in. The filly had been turned out with her halter on and she attempted to scratch an itch on the right side of her face with her right hind foot, something we have all seen horses do. She got her back foot caught in the halter, and in the panic that ensued, she tore off her right ear, poked out her right eye, and destroyed the nerves in her right jaw. She had to be put down.

I have had people call me and ask me to come to their barns to help them catch colts that they put halters on as weanlings when they were small enough to be man-handled. Afterwards, colts could not be caught to get the halters off, and as they grew, the halters just got tighter and tighter. These colts' halters were so tight that their skin had grown around them and they could barely open their mouths to eat or drink. The horses had to be tranquilized so we could cut the halters off.

Even more common is the horse turned out to pasture with his halter on that attempts to scratch his face on the nearest fence post. He either cuts himself in the wire or breaks his neck struggling to free his halter from the fence post. Oh, and let's not forget the horse thieves that are still out there. They just love gentle horses wearing halters in unattended pastures. It makes their job a lot easier.

Take the time to teach your horse to be caught, even if it is only with your belt around his neck or with a hay string you found on your way out to the pasture. Take the time to remove his halter before you turn him loose out in the pasture. It could save his life.

MY HORSE HAS A BAD HABIT OF SLINGING HIS HEAD. HOW CAN I MAKE HIM STOP?

Horses that sling their heads are usually trying to tell you something is wrong. It will not get any better if you lose your cool and jerk the bridle reins. If your horse is slinging his head, listen to him and figure out what he is saying. There are other rare physical problems that can result in head slinging such as eye problems, or problems with his ears so don't hesitate to check with your veterinarian. Don't let your pride get in the way of talking to your veterinarian, as there are many physical reasons that a horse might start head slinging.

Wolf-teeth that haven't been pulled can create a great deal of pain when a hard metal bit bangs against them. Tongues that have been cut by thoughtless or abusive handling will cause a horse to sling his head. A horse can pick up burrs in his mouth while he is grazing. He may have molars that need attention. You may be using a bit that is not right for your horse.

When people ask about the correct bit for their horse, I ask them if their horse has a low or a high palate, a thick or thin tongue, a deep or shallow mouth, thick or thin refined lips. They often have no idea why, or what difference it makes.

Get someone who knows the mechanics of bits and the anatomy of the horse's mouth to help you select one that will be most compatible with your horse and what you are trying to teach him. Don't pick out a bit because it is engraved real pretty or because it's cheap. Read about bits and their functions before you make your final selection.

My good friend Greg Darnall from Lone Oak, Texas, is a leading authority on bits. He has written a book titled Bits and Bitting that I recommend. He also lectures at equine seminars across the country. I still call Greg for advice when I have a question. You never get too old or too smart to ask questions, especially when it comes to the well-being of your horse.

Once you have checked out all the possibilities for head slinging and you still have not found a logical explanation, look to yourself for the answer. The horse may simply be telling you to quit pulling on his mouth. Ease up and relax. Don't bang around on his mouth and insult his intelligence. He knows what the problem is and he will tell you if you give him the opportunity. Remember: The best "bit" you can have is a bit more knowledge.

WHAT ARE YOUR FEELINGS ABOUT IMPRINTING?

I hear a lot of comments about imprinting. People tell me that they have imprinted their colts and that I should have no problem starting them under saddle. They feel that because when this colt was born they were the ones drying him off, rubbing him all over and sticking their fingers in the foal's nose, mouth, ears, or any other place that seemed appropriate to stick their fingers, he should be ready for anything humans present to him for the rest of his life. I am asked this question at every one of my clinics and it always leaves me in a dilemma as to how to answer. Perhaps the best way to answer this question is by giving a couple of examples.

I have been asked why I never use a bosal on my horse and don't recommend its use at my clinics. I do use bosals at home and I really like them, but I am not expert at using them. If I used one at my clinics, people would get the impression that they are simple to use and everyone should run out and get one. It is not always easy to teach "do as I say, not as I do."

I have had the opportunity to meet some top hackamore reinsmen. They are few and far between. Dick Pieper of Oklahoma is a top reining horse trainer and considered one of the best in the world at using a hackamore. I have been fortunate enough to watch him train young horses and visit with him on the proper use of the hackamore. I have learned by observing him that the distance between knowing what to do with a hackamore and the application of that knowledge, along with developing the feel needed to apply the knowledge correctly, is so great that most people never make the trip.

Even the type of bosal or hackamore is important. You can't go pick up a rawhide cable-core bosal at the local feed store for ten bucks and go home with the idea that as soon as you make your horse's nose and jaw really good and sore you will have a hackamore horse. It doesn't work that way. It takes time and practice to develop the timing and feel required to be successful with a hackamore and most people aren't willing to invest the time or the effort.

Too many people are seeking instant gratification. They go buy the cheap, heavy, rough bosal, tie some cotton rope on the heel knot, climb on, and start jerking and pulling. Their horse gets tired of it, takes his head and runs off to the back side of the pasture with his terrified rider thinking, "See if I ever listen to that Sam Powell again!" That is the reason why, as a rule, I don't advise people to use a hackamore. It is also the reason I don't recommend that people imprint their foals.

The idea behind imprinting is to have a horse that is bonded with humans. It is supposed to desensitize the foal to things he would naturally fear. The problem I have with imprinting is not the imprinting itself; it is with most of the people who attempt it. They don't understand enough about the concept. They apply it haphazardly and create more problems than they solve. Horses that have been improperly imprinted are desensitized to everything. They are dull and difficult to teach.

If you aren't willing to take the time to read the entire book on imprinting and make sure you understand every word and reason, you will create more problems than you will have the desire to deal with farther down the road. If you can't keep from fast-forwarding that video to the interesting parts, then don't undertake the project of imprinting your foal.

It's like brain surgery. I have nothing against it as long as the person doing it understands everything about what he is doing and the consequences of doing it wrong. The people who try to short-cut the process and then have problems with their foal always try to blame the problems on the imprinting rather than on their application of the theory. This is a great disservice to the people who have spent years researching and developing the technique. But, it is for this reason that I prefer not to work with a colt that has been imprinted.

WHAT ABOUT TRIMMING HORSES' EARS AND MUZZLES?

I have a really great gelding that I use at my clinics whose name is Bar S Fairly Dry, affectionately known as Rooster. He gets a lot of attention because of his great looks. People are always commenting about what a beautiful horse he is, and I have to agree with them. Rooster is not a barn horse; he runs in the pasture with the rest of the horses and gets cockleburs in his tail, stick tights in his mane, and mud all over from lying in the creek and rolling in the dirt. He is happy, content, and always ready to go when we travel.

I keep his bridle path clipped, but am often asked why I don't clip the whiskers on his muzzle, the long hair around his eyes and the hair in his ears. Sometimes it seems humans are so concerned with appearances that they overlook what really matters, and the horse suffers.

What good is a saddle that is carved and has engraved silver conchos and glistens under the arena lights if it makes your horse so sore he can't walk the next day? Why do you want that bit that is all engraved if it pinches your horse's mouth every way possible? To me, clipping is in the same category.

I have not been able to find any useless parts in the horse's construction, including his hair, anywhere on his body. Whiskers are there for a purpose. They keep the horse from sticking his nose someplace it doesn't belong. (Kind of makes you wonder why we don't have them too, doesn't it?) Like a cat's whiskers that prevent him from sticking his head someplace he can't get it out of, the horse's whiskers are his feeler gauges. The long hairs around his eyes help keep him from getting too close to something that might poke him in the eye. Remember, I told you horses don't see things real well. The next time you are at a show, look at all the beautiful show horses all clipped and shiny, and notice how many of them have scrapes, scratches, or old, healed-up scars on their faces. The hairs in the horse's ears are like the filters on your air conditioner. They keep dust, dirt and other things that don't belong in his ear from going down his ear canal. Incidentally, where do you think those tiny particles of hair go as you are running those clippers around inside his ear? (Did you say you have a problem with head slinging?)

At a recent horsemanship clinic I was sitting on Rooster watching the students riding around warming up their horses. Rooster had his morning bath, his bridle path clipped, and his feet cleaned out, but he still had all his whiskers and such. A young lady rode by on her on a show horse that was clipped bare on his face and ears and coated with what looked like baby oil. His mane was braided with pretty little bows and his saddle was a real work of art, but it did not come even close to fitting him properly. It reminded me of someone wearing a hat two sizes too small. It was just sitting up on his back and looked as though it would roll off either side if the rider didn't sit up straight. The horse's tail was braided and stuffed into one of those nylon bags that dragged on the ground.

I looked at this girl and her decked out horse and then down at ol' Rooster standing there all calm and cool with his head down waiting to go to work. I remember thinking that maybe we should have dressed up a little bit more before coming to town.

It was a hot day and the flies were really bad in this arena. Every time this horse swished at a fly with his pink nylon tail bag, it sounded like a bass drum. Then he swished a little too high and hit the young lady upside the head with his bag and knocked her new hat into the dirt. It scared her, so she screamed and jerked on her horse's mouth, which scared him. The horse jumped sideways and the young lady with her new clothes and fancy saddle rolled off to one side. She got dumped in the dirt and the saddle ended up under the horse's belly.

Rooster and I went to catch the spooked horse and retrieve what was left of her saddle, and I spent most of the rest of the day trying to convince these up-and-coming young horse people to spend more time concentrating on the things that really matter and to put less emphasis on making statements, verbal or nonverbal.

WHY DO YOU LAY THE HORSE DOWN AT YOUR CLINICS?

A lot has been written lately about the practice of laying a horse down—some pro and some con. In the book *The Horse Whisperer* Tom Booker lays

I lay the horse down to teach him that he does not need to protect himself because I will do that for him. Horse owned by Lane Carter.

I am not about to let any harm come to any horse I am working with, through me or anyone else, and the horse now knows it too.

a horse down and it seems to have everybody passing judgment, writing terrible articles, making speeches, and asking questions about it. I have been asked about it a lot: how I do it, when I do it, and why I do it.

To start with, in all honesty, I do use the practice. However, you must understand that when I say I lay a horse down I mean I lay him down. I do not throw him down, and the technique does not involve the use of a trip rope whereby the horse's foot is yanked out from under him at a flying gallop across the arena. I set it up so the horse decides, after a short time, that it is just easier to lie down than it is to stand right then. He makes the decision.

I don't lay every horse down. I use the technique on horses that have trouble accepting things and trusting me, or that have a hard time staying in one place long enough to think about what I am trying to teach them.

When you lay a horse down, you put him in the most vulnerable position possible for a prey animal. When you lay a horse down he thinks he is going to die because he can't get up to protect himself from you and all the other predators that he thinks are going to come over and feast on his soft, vulnerable underside. That gives me the opportunity to teach him that he does not need to protect himself, because I will do it for him. I tell him I know he is in a bad way, but that he can relax because I am here to protect him. It is not a forcing tool; it is a teaching tool. I rub around on him and touch him all over until he relaxes and sighs, and then I let him up. If the technique is done correctly the horse will realize that his human counterpart is not an enemy to be feared, but a protector to be trusted. When he was at his most vulnerable, this person protected him.

I do not give instruction on the technique and I do not include this technique in any of my videos because, in the wrong hands, it can be used to destroy that which I seek to build with my horses. It can be used as a terrorist technique to force the horse to submit. That is not what I am about. I do not want anyone to use the technique for the wrong reasons and honestly say they learned it from me.

If used by someone who does not know what they are doing, laying a horse down can have deadly consequences. When you have his foot up, if he rears up and you fail to give his foot back to him before he comes down he could break his leg when his weight comes down on the bent leg.

WHAT ABOUT THE USE OF PROTECTIVE BOOTS?

Protective boots are a confusing subject at best. Most of the time they make the horse owner feel better than they do the horse. I often see horses on trail rides wearing protective boots. When I ask the owners why they are using them, they tell me it is to protect their horses' legs, but they are never able to tell me what they are trying to protect them from. They go for a nice long trail ride, and never get out of a walk. They ride through creeks, mud holes, and up dusty trails and these boots fill up with water, mud, sand, leaves and twigs and start chafing the horses' cannon bones, flexor tendons, and fetlocks.

How long do you keep your own boots on after you have waded across

I use boots on my horse during demonstrations to make his dark legs easier to see.

the creek and they have filled up with water, mud, guppies, and Lord knows what else? How comfortable do you think you would be if you had to walk a hundred yards back to the truck before you could take them off? You would probably be cussing every step of the way. Well, your horse feels the same way.

I don't wrap my horse's legs when I trailer him, because I don't drive like a Nascar driver when he is in the trailer. I am always aware of the fact that he is back there and I want his ride to be as comfortable as I can make it.

In the hot summer, boots are particularly aggravating. I have had the opportunity to wear plaster casts on my legs on several different occasions during the summer. My legs would get hot and start sweating. Little beads of sweat would roll down into the cast and my legs would itch like mad, but I couldn't scratch. It's the same for your horse when you trailer him in hot weather wearing shipping boots.

This might tell you why he just won't stand still back there and seems bent on kicking the side out of your new gooseneck trailer. Think about your horse a little. Don't do something to your horse because your neighbor does it to his. Don't use a product because you think it looks real neat. Think about what you are doing before you do it. Be practical and you will find understanding your horse is not really that difficult. In fact it's pretty simple.

I do use boots on my horse during demonstrations because they make his dark legs easier to see as I am explaining. They are for aesthetic purposes only. If you feel you need to use the boots on your horse for protection, ask yourself these questions: If my horse needs these boots to protect him from injury while I am working him, what should I be doing differently? In other words, are you causing your horse to injure himself because you are asking him to do something he does not know how to do? Is he conformationally incapable of doing what you are asking? For example, a reining horse that constantly steps on himself as he is learning to spin may not be conformationally correct enough to cross over himself in the front. This horse will always need protection, but a better solution is to find a different program he can fit into. If this same horse is stepping on himself because he is just too lazy to pick his feet up and cross over himself, protective boots keep him from being uncomfortable, so there is no incentive for him to get it right.

The answer goes back to knowing and understanding your horse and your ultimate goal. I do agree with the use of the boots on a reining horse that stops hard and deep. Without boots there is a tendency for the horse to be burned by the ground when he slides. It only takes a couple of burns before the horse does not want to stop, and a reiner that won't slide long, hard, and deep will not make it in competition.

WHAT ABOUT LUNGEING?

I don't work my horse on a lunge line unless it is absolutely necessary. I would rather turn him into an arena or round pen and let him exercise himself than work him on a lunge line because it is hard on the horse. He goes around in a little twenty- or thirty-foot circle, driving off his inside hind leg with his body in an arc, dropping his inside shoulder and pulling his face to the outside of the circle. None of these are desirable traits you want your horse to have once you get on and start riding. Free lungeing in a sixty-foot round pen lets him get exercise, stay squared up in the front end, and drive himself off of both hind legs as he was designed to do.

If you have to lunge on a line, don't hang onto the horse's head constantly. Give him some slack. If he gets out of round then bump him back where you want him to be and get out of his face again. You don't want him to learn to pull on your hands when you're riding him. Neither do you want him to get in the habit of looking away from you when you are working him.

When getting ready to stop him, don't holler "Whoa" and yank his head toward you. Tell him to whoa, let him get stopped, and then turn him to you. If you tell him to whoa and pull his head at the same time he will start planting his inside front foot and swinging his butt away from you. Then, when you are riding him you will wonder why, when you ask him to stop and pull on his face, he stops on his front end and throws you over the saddle horn.

Don't spend time teaching your horse things on a lunge line that you will have to teach him to forget when you get on his back.

HOW DO YOU FEEL ABOUT THE USE OF AUTOMATIC WATERERS IN A HORSE STALL?

I like to have a pretty good idea of how much water my horse consumes during the day, so I use buckets in his stall and small tanks in the pasture. Sometimes these are a lot of trouble, but my horse is worth it. Using a small tank that I have to fill every day encourages me to dump and clean it before putting in fresh water. If I use a big water tank that I only need to fill once a week, by that time there are things growing and dead varmints floating in it, and I don't know whether the horses drank the water or it has evaporated.

When I am on the road I carry my own water buckets. I don't use the deep, five-gallon buckets. Horses will generally only drink down until their eyes are level with the top of the bucket. They don't like putting their heads down farther because they're too claustrophobic. So you always have water left in the bucket and, if you're like most people, instead of dumping it and adding fresh, you just add clean water to what is already there. If you do dump the water, you're wasting about two gallons of water each time you refill the bucket.

If I lay over during a road trip and stable my horses at a barn that has automatic waterers, I turn them off, dip them out and use my own water buckets. Automatic waterers that have consumption meters on them are fine, but if my horse goes off water I want to know about it right away before the problem gets serious. A horse that goes off water can get seriously ill very quickly.

If you do use automatic waterers, take time to check and clean them often because horses dribble feed and hay and bacteria grow in them. A horse will not drink out of a water fountain that has a dead mouse in it. For the health of your horse, try to come up with some means by which you can measure his water consumption. Sometimes we do so much to make life easier on ourselves that we sacrifice the health and well-being of the very animals we claim to care so much about.

Left: Fairhill Enterprise, Bar S Quarter Horses, Denton, Texas. Horse owned by Mark Schrimpf. *Photo © Waltenberry, Inc.*

Below, right: Bar S Pine Bar (Sneaker). Bar S stallions are selected for their minds, their conformation, and their athletic ability. Horse owned by Mark Schrimpf. *Photo © Waltenberry, Inc.*

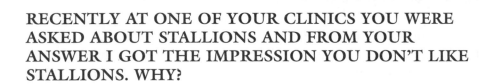

RECENTLY AT ONE OF YOUR CLINICS YOU WERE ASKED ABOUT STALLIONS AND FROM YOUR ANSWER I GOT THE IMPRESSION YOU DON'T LIKE STALLIONS. WHY?

First of all, I have absolutely nothing against stallions. The problem I have is with a lot of the people who own them. Traveling the country as we do, we meet a lot of stallions and their owners. Many of these stallions won't even make good geldings, but the owner continues to breed them year after year. Stallions are the base for improving our breeds and people who breed stallions that have no real conformation quality and no athletic ability pass those same faults on to their offspring year after year.

At a clinic last year, a lady asked my advice about her stallion. She told me he wasn't much to look at, hadn't done much, didn't come from any outstanding bloodlines, and did not have much in the way of talent—in fact, he was a little clumsy. She said he could be mean at times, but that she wanted to breed him to a few mares to increase his value. That attitude bothers me! How could you possibly think that breeding an inferior stallion that produces inferior foals would, in any way, make that stallion more valuable? People who want to own and breed stallions because they want to "raise little babies" make me shudder.

It scares me to see people handling stallions who have no clue about the danger involved. Remember, in Chapter One I said that stallions are born with two objectives: breeding and fighting. If you don't consider the stallion's mental makeup you can very quickly put yourself in harm's way.

There are exceptions to every rule, of course, and we have all seen wonderfully behaved stallions at horse shows, on television, and lots of other places. What most people don't realize, though, is what it took to make those stallions so well-mannered. Most people are not willing to take the program far enough and put forth the effort necessary to achieve this result.

First, it takes a stallion that has a lot of intelligence and wants to learn. He has to want to get along with you and go along with your program. It has to be his decision, because, ultimately you will lose any battle you engage in with a stallion. Second, you have to be intelligent enough to recognize these qualities and to recognize the fact that not all horses have them. Again, if you are too busy looking for the good to see the obvious bad, then you aren't seeing the truth.

Bar S stallions, for example, are selected for their minds, their conformation, and their athletic ability. Without all three, the horse doesn't meet the criteria to remain a stallion.

Last year I was at the Bar S during breeding season and Mark was showing his stallions to some visitors. He had just brought Fairhill Enterprise into the breeding barn to be collected for artificial insemination. Some people there mentioned how well-behaved he was and wanted to know how he rode. Mark led Fairhill into the indoor arena, jumped on him bareback with only a halter to guide him, and proceeded to lope circles, do spins, and sliding stops. It takes a knowledgeable handler and a very special stallion to be able to do this. These are the only types of stallions that should be bred—the really outstanding ones.

Another of Mark's stallions, Lena's Gyrator, was retired for four years. In preparation for the upcoming United States Equestrian Team events he has been put back into a conditioning program. The first day he was saddled after not having been ridden for four years, the rider stepped aboard Gyrator and rode off, loping circles and doing sliding stops like he had never been out of training a day in his life.

If you are going to breed stallions, do so with the goal of improving the quality of your particular breed, and not just to raise babies. Take the time to search for and select only those horses that meet the strictest criteria. Stallions selected for breeding should be bright, intelligent, conformationally correct according to the breed's standard, and willing to learn. In my opinion too many people are keeping studs and breeding them who have no business doing either. For the sake of breed improvement, I think we as horse owners should be more selective and discriminating with the stallions whose genes we choose to pass on to future generations.

If you are not sure if your stallion meets your breed's standards, by all means ask a professional. In reality, though, if you have to ask, you have not studied enough stallions and you're not quite ready to be a breeder.

MY HORSE NICKERS AT THE OTHER HORSES WHILE I AM WORKING WITH HIM. HOW CAN I GET HIM TO STOP?

First of all, I wouldn't get too upset about it, but if it became a real problem then I would try to correct it. Horses are very social animals, as I have already mentioned, and nickering to other horses can mean a number of different things. Before you assume it is a problem, find out whether it was just two neighbors greeting each other or if it was a challenge to another horse to fight. If you are riding a stallion, is he just flexing his manly muscles trying to impress the girls?

I believe that most of the problems we encounter with horses can be traced back to lack of basic training, mainly not enough respect for the rider. If you have that respect, not only do you have the ability to prevent problems from ever getting started, you also have the means to correct those that do. You need to have enough basic foundation on your horse to direct his attention where you need it and to direct his feet where you want them. If your horse nickers, just direct his attention somewhere else and direct his feet to give him something to do. Don't get in a fight with him by jerking on his mouth or poking him with a spur. Think about what he is doing, and ask yourself if it is worth getting worked up over.

WHAT'S HORSE WHISPERING ALL ABOUT? IS IT A GIFT?

Ever since the release of Nicholas Evans' best selling novel, *The Horse Whisperer*, there has been much propaganda surrounding the age-old practice known as horse whispering.

A Z-donk that I successfully used my Teaching by Asking techniques on in 1994.

Fortunately, the mass media attention has brought some much-deserved recognition to those master horsemen who quietly and unassumingly go about their business of improving the quality of life for horses on a daily basis. This media attention has put the work of the Ray Hunts, the Tom Dorrances, and the Buck Branamans at the forefront of a widening movement that has horse people everywhere, novices and professionals alike, rethinking and restructuring their relationships with horses.

Unfortunately, this same media attention has nearly every semi-competent horseman claiming to be *the* Horse Whisperer, along with some incompetent ones as well. Suddenly it seems as though no one refers to them as trainers, horsemen, or even cowboys any more. Even in a positive light it is confusing at best to try to understand just what a horse whisperer is.

A recent publication of an article titled "Horse Whisperer or Horse Feathers" (*Horse and Rider*, Feb. 1999) worried me that the alleged deception of the public by one man claiming to be *the* Horse Whisperer will cast a shadow of doubt upon the ability of the true master horsemen who honestly and earnestly practice kinder, gentler methods of working with their horses.

How ironic that I should feel compelled to defend those horsemen who, in reality, neither need nor want to be defended. These men are what they are and profess to be nothing more. Most of them consider themselves to be just cowboys. Whatever they call themselves, they possess the cowboy integrity that went a long way in forming the traditional values

Fairhill Enterprise. It takes a special stallion to be able to demonstrate the intelligence, talent, looks, and manners that the Bar S stallions do even during the breeding season. *Photo © Waltenberry, Inc.*

that made this country. These men are motivated by a desire to educate the world about a better way of working with horses.

Perhaps the best way to defend those whom the media refers to as horse whisperers is by taking the mystery out of horse whispering. Although little is known about these eccentric equestrians prior to the sixteenth century, some believe they were lineal descendants of the privileged military horse handlers of medieval times.

The term itself creates an air of mystery and romanticism for those who seek such things. There are those who prefer to believe the whisperers' talents with the horses are the result of magic or stem from supernatural powers rather than the result of many years of hard work and dedication. Perhaps it was this kind of thinking that caused the whisperers' self-imposed secrecy in the beginning in order to avoid charges of witchcraft. It makes sense to me that their secrecy, while for their own protection, further fueled the notion that the practice had to do with magic, sorcery, or witchcraft.

While the Oxford English Dictionary refers to a horse whisperer as an appellation for certain celebrated horse breakers said to have obtained obedience by whispering to horses, I prefer to use the much broader and more generic, but more accurate, description given in Chapter Two of this book.

It is doubtful that we could research back far enough to determine exactly who was the first horse whisperer. We do know that there is not the Horse Whisperer, but there are the horse whisperers, plural. It is not so much a title as it is a practice. All horse whisperers are not the same, just as all doctors and all preachers are not the same. It may be true that all doctors and all preachers ultimately have the same end goal of their chosen profession in mind, but it is not true that they are all the same, or even that they use the same methods and techniques to achieve that goal.

It is your perception and interpretation of the man and his methods that makes one whisperer better than another. If you attend a seminar or clinic conducted by a horseman that you relate to, understand very well, and agree with, then chances are you will consider him to be the better horseman than the one whose presentation was more difficult for you to understand.

The true master horsemen are those who are not so interested in showing you what they can do with your horse as they are in showing you what you can do with him and teaching you how to do it. Because they care so much for the horses, they realize that the only way they can achieve their ultimate goal of a better quality of life for horses is by teaching other people to do what they do. Don't misunderstand me—there is no way that a person can learn in a few short weeks what it has taken the teacher a lifetime to learn. In a few short weeks, though, you can be well on your way to learning to think about how to get the most from your horse based on a better understanding of him. Taking in a student for a period of twelve weeks and trying to cover a lifetime of knowledge and experience and then telling the student he is certified is not fair to the student or to those he will teach farther down the road. Twelve weeks of training doesn't make a person certified, a whisperer, or even a horseman.

The truth is that horse whispering has absolutely nothing to do with magic, potions, talismans, charms, trinkets, voodoo, mental telepathy, hats with moveable ears, or whispering. What it does have to do with is a deep, intimate understanding of the horse, his nature, and his culture. Nearly all the true master horsemen have spent their entire lifetimes observing and learning about horses. Most would probably tell you they still have a lot to learn about the horses and about being able to distinguish between love for them and understanding of them.

Horse whisperers understand the horse well enough to establish effective lines of communication, rather than chains of command. They communicate with the horse by mimicking his body language. Once this line of communication has been opened up, truly remarkable seemingly magical things can happen, often in a short period of time. These master horsemen have so great an understanding of the horse that it has become not a second nature to them, but incorporated into their primary nature. Understanding the horse is as natural to the horse whisperer as breathing.

Horse whispering can and often does have to do with a great deal of love and respect for horses, but it has more to do with the realization that love and respect are not nearly as effective alone as when they are coupled with the ability to understand and communicate with him. Without understanding, there can be no communication.

To most of the world, the language of the horse is very soft and subtle, almost imperceptible. Perhaps this is the true origin of the term "whisperer," for their language is indeed almost a whisper. Once you really understand horses, they speak loud and clear. I personally know of no horse whisperer who actually whispers to his horses. Most of them make a lot of noise when they work, and they do it on purpose.

Horse whispering also has to do with simplicity, because the language of the horse is a simple one. It is also universal. Horses all over the world speak the same language and the same word means the same thing every time. There is no reading between the lines and no trying to figure out if Horse said what he meant and meant what he said. Horses are brutally honest, and you can't get any simpler than that. Horse whispering is not easy, but it is not complicated. Yes, I did say it is not easy, since it is often difficult to learn because it takes much time and effort.

Referring to horse whisperers as "gifted" implies a belief that no effort has been put forth by the whisperer to develop his talent. Most of the master horsemen I know have attended the school of hard knocks and practical application for many, many years. They have learned what works largely by learning what does not—the hard way. If whispering were to be considered a gift, most horsemen I know would consider it to be the most expensive gift they ever received and paid for out of their own pockets.

Horse whispering is also to a large extent about perception, sensitivity, and skill. There are people who have the ability to demonstrate these same traits with other animals and with people. I hope that if there is ever a dog whisperer or people whisperer trend, folks will make more effort to fully understand and appreciate the talents and efforts of the whisperers rather than assuming they possess some supernatural power. In short, horse whisperers are ordinary people who have developed an extraordinary understanding of the horse through years of hard work and observation and who now put their knowledge to work creating better lives for horses. They should be admired and respected for that.

Afterword

If I could have but one wish in life, it would be to spend one more day with my Dad, not to show him all I *have* learned, but for all I still have *to* learn about horses and about people. One thing I know: the true horseperson *never* stops learning.

I have summed up what my life is about in the form of my company's mission statement, and I live by it every day. It is: Dedicated to promoting responsible ownership and enjoyment of horses by novices and professionals alike by establishing effective lines of communication rather than chains of command. Working to improve the quality of life for horses by educating their owners on any equine-related subject or connecting them to the most qualified professionals in that field.

I want to put the burden of responsible horse ownership back where it belongs . . . on the people who own the horse. Anyone can be an owner, but it takes work and a willingness to learn in order to be a *responsible* owner. The answers I give people and the concepts that I teach are not always the most popular, but they are always truth based on what is best for the horse. And what is best for the horse is, in the long run, best for you, too.

Sources of Information

Sam Powell Equine Consulting Services, Inc.
P.O. Box 892
Hendersonville, TN 37077-0892
615-826-2826

University of Tennessee
Agricultural Extension Service
5201 Marchant Dr.
Nashville, TN 37211
615-832-8341

Purina Mills, Inc.
P.O. Box 66812
St. Louis, MO 63166-6812
Customer Service 1-800-227-8941

Bar S Quarter Horses
Mark Schrimpf
P.O. Box 307
Denton, TX 76202
940-482-3186

American Association of Equine Practitioners
4075 Iron Works Pike
Lexington, KY 40511
606-233-0147

American Horse Council
1700 K St. NW, Suite 300
Washington, DC 20006
202-296-4031
(call for the location of your state Horse Council)

American Farrier's Association
4059 Iron Works Pk., Suite 2
Lexington, KY 40511
606-233-7411

Horse Industry Alliance
8314 White Settlement Rd.
Ft. Worth, TX 76116
817-246-7433

About the Author

SAM POWELL is a former rodeo cowboy, federal livestock inspector, and Oklahoma ranch manager who now resides in the Nashville, Tennessee, area. He operates a full-scale equine consulting service and travels the world conducting teaching clinics to help people learn how to better communicate with their horses and each other. His method, known as Teaching by Asking, is becoming increasingly more popular as people seek a more humane approach to working with horses.

Sam has spent his entire lifetime studying and learning about horses as beings with a culture of their own. As a boy he observed horses in the wild in the mountains of Arizona and Nevada, but it would be many years before he put what he learned there into practical application. Using traditional methods of breaking horses and spending several years on the rodeo circuit, Sam saw more than his share of horses with cuts, bruises, broken bones, and broken spirits. Having nearly every bone in his own body broken at one time or another, some more than once, prompted him to seek a better way of working with horses. A spiritual transformation helped him find it.

As he recalled the teachings of his father and the horses he had observed over the years, Sam reconfigured things in his head and the resulting theory made sense, at least hypothetically. Gradually he put the theory into practical application and it worked. As he transformed his thinking about horses, he found himself rethinking the things he knew about people and putting these theories into practical application, too. To his surprise, they also worked. Thus, he has begun to rediscover and appreciate the traditional values that made this country. Discovery of a kinder, gentler method of working with horses has yielded a kinder, gentler man.

Sam has spent the past ten years perfecting his technique and teaching it to others. He has been referred to as a Horse Whisperer by the media and those to whom he lectures. He has traveled to Germany, Australia, and Hawaii to teach his methods. Since moving to the Nashville area, his list of clients has grown to include many people in the country music industry. His clinic audiences include all types of horsepeople, from the backyard equine enthusiasts to feedlot cowboys who make their living on horseback

Sam maintains a one-on-one approach with an emphasis on honesty, fairness, and simplicity. He hopes this book will be seen as an extension of that approach.

Index